Alvina Habib

RDBMS vs ORDBMS vs NoSQL

Alvina Habib

RDBMS vs ORDBMS vs NoSQL

LAP LAMBERT Academic Publishing

Impressum / Imprint

Bibliografische Information der Deutschen Nationalbibliothek: Die Deutsche Nationalbibliothek verzeichnet diese Publikation in der Deutschen Nationalbibliografie; detaillierte bibliografische Daten sind im Internet über http://dnb.d-nb.de abrufbar.
Alle in diesem Buch genannten Marken und Produktnamen unterliegen warenzeichen-, marken- oder patentrechtlichem Schutz bzw. sind Warenzeichen oder eingetragene Warenzeichen der jeweiligen Inhaber. Die Wiedergabe von Marken, Produktnamen, Gebrauchsnamen, Handelsnamen, Warenbezeichnungen u.s.w. in diesem Werk berechtigt auch ohne besondere Kennzeichnung nicht zu der Annahme, dass solche Namen im Sinne der Warenzeichen- und Markenschutzgesetzgebung als frei zu betrachten wären und daher von jedermann benutzt werden dürften.

Bibliographic information published by the Deutsche Nationalbibliothek: The Deutsche Nationalbibliothek lists this publication in the Deutsche Nationalbibliografie; detailed bibliographic data are available in the Internet at http://dnb.d-nb.de.
Any brand names and product names mentioned in this book are subject to trademark, brand or patent protection and are trademarks or registered trademarks of their respective holders. The use of brand names, product names, common names, trade names, product descriptions etc. even without a particular marking in this work is in no way to be construed to mean that such names may be regarded as unrestricted in respect of trademark and brand protection legislation and could thus be used by anyone.

Coverbild / Cover image: www.ingimage.com

Verlag / Publisher:
LAP LAMBERT Academic Publishing
ist ein Imprint der / is a trademark of
OmniScriptum GmbH & Co. KG
Heinrich-Böcking-Str. 6-8, 66121 Saarbrücken, Deutschland / Germany
Email: info@lap-publishing.com

Herstellung: siehe letzte Seite /
Printed at: see last page
ISBN: 978-3-659-68097-7

Zugl. / Approved by: London, University of Hertfordshire, 2014

Abstract

Relational and Non-relational models are the emerging models which are being implemented in industries these days. They are extremely different from each other in terms of performance, design, modelling etc.

The huge amounts of data consumption (big data) is becoming a huge problem day by day due to storage technologies not evolving fast enough to provide the efficient performance needed.

This dissertation investigates the performance (in terms of speed (runtime) and memory usage) of three Database Management Systems (DBMSs) i-e Object Relational (PostgreSQL), Relational (SQL) and Non-relational/NoSQL (MongoDB) Databases using "Airline Information System" (Elmasri, 2011) case study. This report aims to analyze and compare three databases and to address the research question whether one performs better than the other and are there any significant differences in their performance.

By comparison, I investigated the strengths and weaknesses of all three DBMSs e.g in RDBMSs there is a schema (ERD) to design and model database but in NoSQL databases there is no such schema, for this purpose I have designed my own schema and presented it in the section 5.2.3 of this report. Runtime and memory needed to carry out queries of varying degree of complexity using PostgreSQL, SQL and MongoDB Database systems have been measured and statistically analyzed. For this purpose, I applied one-factor and two-factor **analysis of variance (ANOVA)** on queries' runtimes, but I didn't apply any statistics on memory usage due to little or no variance within groups and I have analyzed memory usage on the basis of data using PostgreSQL, SQL and MongoDB Database systems.

The conclusion of the report is based on the results of **ANOVA** that have been explained in chapter 7 and chapter 8, briefly the conclusion is "**MongoDB is fastest Database in performance (in terms of speed (runtime) and memory usage). On the other hand, SQL Database is slowest in terms of speed (runtime) and PostgreSQL Database is worst in memory consumption**".

0

Acknowledgement

I have made this attempt to achieve the goal that was set for me to complete the MS degree. Although the project was complex and complicated, I put my maximum effort to fulfill the goal. However, it would have been impossible without the kind support and help of my Supervisor **Rene Te Boekhorst**. I would like to extend my sincere gratitude to him for his guidance and constant supervision as well as for providing necessary information and support regarding the project & also for his assistance in improving the project.

Table of Contents

1.1.   Introduction

Efficient storage and recovery of data has always been a question to ponder over due to everyday growing needs. Larger amounts of data transactions require organized storage technologies. Databases were created with the purpose to fulfill growing needs of data storage and retrieval in a well-organized way. Two of the most popular database systems are relational databases and NoSQL databases. Although NoSQL databases are relatively new, but they are emerging due to their ability to handle unstructured data quickly, primarily because they do not require a fixed schema and complex operations like joins, also they are flexible (Education Portal, 2014).

The primary concept of my project is to address the following research question: **"Are there any significant differences in performance (in terms of speed (runtime) and memory usage)w.r.t query type complexity and DB Size between Object-Relational DBMS (PostgreSql), Relational DBMS (SQL) and Document-Oriented NoSQL (Mongo dB) DBMS?"**

For the purpose of analysis and comparison of the performance of structured **(PostgreSQL & SQL)** and non-structured or schema- less **(Mongo dB)** databases in terms of runtime and memory usage, a suitable case study "Airline Information System" has been taken from the textbook "Fundamentals of Database Systems" (Elmasri, 2011). In the Advanced Databases (7COM1022) module, I was taught how to setup Entity relationship diagram and then how to map the ERD schema to tables for another case study.

In this project, I designed, modelled and implemented Airline Information System using Object-Relational (PostgreSql), Relational (SQL) and Document-Oriented NoSQL (Mongo dB) DBMSs.

After implementation, 5 queries were designed for three different above mentioned DBMSs and their runtime and memory usages have been documented (Appendix 1, 2 and 3).

I applied two-Factor ANOVA on the datasets of the queries' runtime and memory usage and depending on ANOVA results; I concluded **"MongoDB performs best (in terms of speed (runtime) and memory usage)"**.

4

1.2. Research Question

Are there any significant differences in performance (in terms of speed (runtime) and memory usage) w.r.t query type complexity and DB Size between three database systems Object-Relational (PostgreSQL) DBMS, Relational (SQL) DBMS and Document-Oriented NoSQL (MongoDB) DBMS?

1.3. Hypothesis

There are three Null Hypothesis (H_0) and Alternative Hypothesis (H_A).

1: H_0: There is NO (significant) difference in performance (in terms of speed (runtime) and memory usage) w.r.t Database Size using each of the three database systems i-e Object-Relational (PostgreSQL) DBMS, Relational (SQL) DBMS and Document-Oriented NoSQL (MongoDB) DBMS.**OR** There is NO (significant) difference in the means of the runtime and memory usage w.r.t Database Size i-e **$\mu1= \mu2= \mu3$.**

1: H_A: There is a (significant) difference in performance (in terms of speed (runtime) and memory usage) w.r.t Database Size using each of the three database systems i-e Object-Relational (PostgreSQL) DBMS, Relational (SQL) DBMS and Document-Oriented NoSQL (MongoDB) DBMS.

OR There is (significant) difference in the means of runtime and memory usage i-e **$\mu1\neq \mu2\neq \mu3$.**

2: H_0: There is NO (significant) difference in performance (in terms of speed (runtime) and memory usage) w.r.t query type complexity between three Database Systems i-e Object-Relational DBMS (PostgreSQL) DBMS, Relational (SQL) DBMS and Document-Oriented NoSQL (MongoDB) DBMS.

OR There is NO (significant) difference in the means of runtime and memory usage i-e **$\mu1= \mu2= \mu3$.**

2: H_A: There is a (significant) difference in performance (in terms of speed (runtime) and memory usage) w.r.t query type complexity between three database systems i-e Object-Relational (PostgreSQL) DBMS, Relational (SQL) DBMS and Document-Oriented NoSQL (MongoDB) DBMS.

OR There is a (significant) difference in the means of runtime and memory usage i-e **$\mu1\neq \mu2\neq \mu3$.**

3: H$_0$: There is NO (significant) difference in performance (in terms of speed (runtime) and memory usage) w.r.t query type complexity using each of the three Database Systems Object-Relational (PostgreSQL) DBMS, Relational (SQL) DBMS and Document-Oriented NoSQL (MongoDB) DBMS.

OR There is NO (significant) difference in the means of runtime and memory usage i-e $\mu1 = \mu2 = \mu3 = \mu4 = \mu5$.

3: H$_A$: There is a (significant) difference in performance (in terms of speed (runtime) and memory usage) w.r.t query type complexity using each of the three database systems Object-Relational DBMS (PostgreSql), Relational DBMS (SQL) and Document-Oriented NoSQL (Mongo dB) DBMS.

OR There is (significant) difference in the means of runtime and memory usage w.r.t query type complexity i-e $\mu1 \neq \mu2 \neq \mu3 \neq \mu4 \neq \mu5$.

1.4. Aims

Major aims and goals achieved in my project are:

- Research on Object-Relational (PostgreSQL), Relational (SQL) and Non-Relational (MongoDB) DBMSs.

- Implementation, design and modelling of the Airline Information System case study in (PostgreSQL & SQL) using schema (ERD) and MongoDB using self-designed schema.

- Analysis of the strengths and weaknesses of PostgreSQL, SQL and NoSQL databases.

- Investigation of the performance of three DBMSs. For this purpose, two-factor analysis of variance (**ANOVA**) has been applied on datasets of queries' runtime and memory usage in PostgreSQL, SQL and MongoDB Databases.

- Comparison of the above three databases' performance and to conclude MongoDB performs is better in terms of speed (runtime) and memory usage for the specific case study on the basis of ANOVA statistical results.

1.5. Outline of the Report

The report consists of eight main chapters and the structure is as follows:

- **Chapter 1:** describes the brief introduction, Research Question and Hypothesis. Moreover the Achieved Goals and have also been discussed in this chapter. Outline of the Report concludes this chapter.

6

- **Chapter 2:** displays project management using Gantt chart.

- **Chapter 3:** presents the detailed background of three DBMSs, their literature review, their comparison and some related literature work concludes this chapter.

- **Chapter 4:** provides the case study Airline Information System taken from the text book "Fundamentals of Database Systems by Elmasri 6th Edition".

- **Chapter 5:** details the implementation and modelling of above case study using the three DBMSs i-e Object-Relational (PostgreSQL), Relational (SQL) and NoSQL (MongoDB). This chapter includes physical and logical modelling for PostgreSQL and SQL and self-designed schema MongoDB. It also includes the insertion of data by referencing and embedding documents in MongoDB.

- **Chapter 6:** presents the design, syntax and results of the queries. Moreover, this chapter also includes the most challenging part of my project i-e runtime and memory usage recordings of queries at execution time.

- **Chapter 7:** elaborates the investigation using two-factor ANOVA to test the performance within and between database systems.

- **Chapter 8:** This chapter concludes the project depending of ANOVA statistical results. It also discusses future research that can be done on this project.

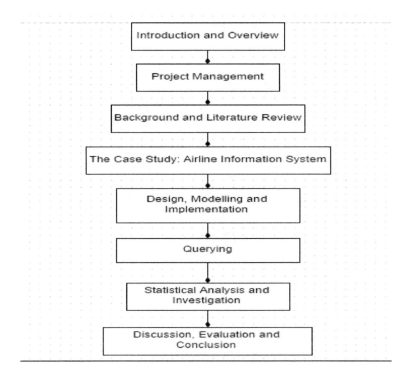

Figure 1: Logical organization of the report and suggested paths through it.

2.1. Gantt chart

One way to represent a project's plan is to use a work breakdown structure (WBS) i-e a technique for splitting tasks into sub-tasks and generating a task hierarchy. For this purpose, I have used Microsoft Project Professional to create Gantt chart which is shown in Figure 2 below:

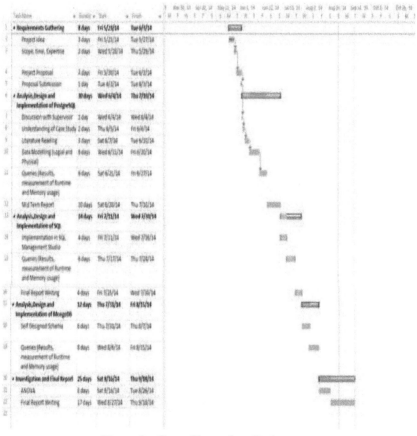

Figure 2 : Gantt Chart of my Project

A database is an organized collection of data in form of tables that simply contain rows and columns. For efficient storage and retrieval of the data items in a database, a Database Management System (DBMS) is used.

DBMS is a set of software/hardware instructions designed for the purpose of handling interaction of an application with the database using a variety of different relational and non-relational data models (Webopedia.com, 2014). There are different types of DBMSs, ranging from standalone systems that run on personal computers to massive systems that work on mainframes.

The following categories of DBMSs can be distinguished:
- Relational Database management systems (SQL)
- Object-Relational Database management systems (PostgreSQL)
- Non-relational Database management systems (NoSQL or Not only SQL)

The evolving landscape of database systems is shown in Figure 3 below (McNulty, 2014):

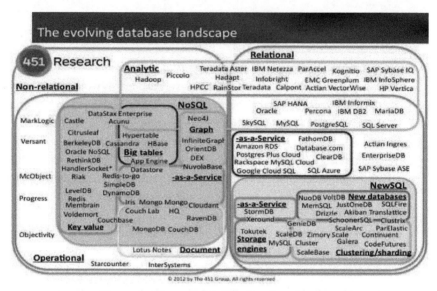

Figure 3: The evolving Database Landscape

3.1.   Relational DBMS

The relational model's simplicity (human readability) and mathematical grounds (relational algebra and relational calculus) are two reasons why it has been the leading DBMS for the past thirty years (Silberschatz, et. Al 2011).

Reliability, concurrency control recovery, durability and data integrity for persistent application are some major features that software engineers keep in mind to design an efficient and maintainable system (Nichols, 2007).

In 1970, Dr. E. F. Codd presented the paper, "*A Relational Model of Data for Large Shared Data Banks*" in the ACM journal (Codd, 1970). Codd's model is now accepted as the definitive model for RDBMS. Since 1970, relational DBMS have been the leading DBMS used in the industry (Docs.oracle.com, 2014).

Following are the three specific components that Codd presented in relational Model (Codd, 1970):

1. **Data structures for data storage**:

Codd described relation/table, attributes/columns, tuples/rows, relation instance, and relation schema/table header as data structures use to store data.

2. **Integrity Constraints:**

11

Integrity constraints like domain, key, referential, procedural (application dependent constraints)

3. **Operations:**

Operations include Relational algebra and relational calculus.

A RDBMS promotes data models such as Entity Relationship Diagrams (ERD) (Nichols, 2007). The primary key and foreign key concepts are very important in RDBMS as they provide a link between tables. SQL (structured query language) is used to communicate with the database (Sqlcourse.com, 2014). SQL is used to query, insert and modify data and most RDBMSs use SQL as standard query language. The language, Structured English Query Language (SEQUEL now called SQL) was developed by IBM Corporation, Inc., to use Codd's model (Docs.oracle.com, 2014). SQL is based on relational algebra and relational calculus. SQL became a standard for ANSI (American National Standards Institute) in 1986 and of ISO (International Organization for Standardization) in 1987(Techopedia.com, 2014).

The most popular RDBMSs are MS SQL, DB2, Oracle and MySQL (Databasedir.com, 2014).

3.2. Object-Relational DBMS

Object oriented databases began to emerge in the mid-80 in response to the feeling that relational databases were insufficient for certain areas of applications (Stajano, 1998). In 1986, Postgres released the first object relational database management system (ORDBMS). ORBBMS technology has been emerging because it provides a way to enhance object-oriented features RDBMSs. (Wang, 2010). At the present, the three leading DBMSs Oracle, IBM and Microsoft have extended their systems to support SQL 2003 standard which takes in object-relational features. Some experts forecast that because of support for ORDMBSs' features from all three above mentioned vendors, in the nearby future ORDBMSs will have a 50% greater stake of the market than the RDBMS market (Connolly et. Al, 2002).

In 1980s, Object relational databases emerged and the vendors of relational databases could not ignore their advent because in relational database one has to normalize data even if it is complex that doesn't make any sense. Consider an example; if there is a need to normalize a bitmapped image which is an ordered list of pixels, it results in a table with pixels as rows and primary key that reflects their order as an attribute. In this case, it is obviously better to save the data as an object. This is the point where ORDBMS became popular. An Object-Relational approach includes objects that need data model, a query language and a DBMS (Bloor, 2003).

The most popular Object-RDBMSs are PostgreSQL, Oracle and CUBRID.

3.3.   Object-Relational vs Relational Databases

Comparison of ORDBMS and RDBMS results in the following distinguished aspects:

- Object-Relational is also relational DBMS with SQL3 extensions and these extensions include user-defined types and routines, inheritance whose major feature is reusability of components, polymorphism i-e the process to present the same interface to different underlying forms (data types), object identity, reference types, collections types like Arrays, encapsulation, ability to create abstract and user defined data types etc (SAB\uAU, 2007) (Ji-feng et. Al, 2004).

- A relational DBMS is regarded as by simple with increased stability as compared to ORDBMS (SAB\uAU, 2007).

- RDBMSs are rigid due to the data storage in the form of tables and they work only with restricted and simple data types, such as integers, vchar etc and thus it is difficult to handle complex and user defined data types, including multimedia (Leavitt, 2000).

- For RDBMS there is SQL2 standard (ANSI X3H2) and for ORDBMS there is SQL3 standard which is advance (SAB\uAU, 2007).

- The primary advantage of ORDBMSs is that unlike RDBMSs, they usually don't need to collect the data beforehand. They lean towards data storage in its most-used form, which usually enhance performance and make the system efficient. ORDBMSs also have ability to implement caching strategies that make it more possible for data to be in memory when it is demanded. They need slight optimization to recover data. As new systems are built, the need to operate complex data like sophisticated graphics; documents, multimedia, web pages etc. are better dealt by ORDBMSs (Bloor, 2003).

- Another major advantage of using ORDBMS is the removal of impedance mismatch between applications and database model. Impedance mismatch is defined by (Egenhofer et. Al, 1992) as "*incompatibilities that occur at each interface between two set of tools due to the different models for importation representation*" (Connolly et. Al, 2002). An impedance mismatch between an application and a database disturbs overall application development performance, time, memory usage and results in

13

discrepancies between the design and the implementation of the application (Egenhofer et. Al, 1992).

- Another advantage of ORDBMS over RDBMS is their ease to model real world objects and the relationships between these objects (Nichols, 2007).

- In RDBMS, relational joins are one of the most expensive operations (Leavitt, 2000).Whereas in an ORDBMS, object references can be used to access related tables instead of complex table joins. It is easier to navigate between objects using the object-oriented dot notation through Object references (Nichols, 2007).

3.4.   Big Data: A Revolution

In today's era, most people are interacting via social networks, various websites and by means of internet; it has become easier to access someone's personal data through third parties such as Facebook, Google+, LinkedIn, Yahoo etc. This isn't something that only concerns so-called above mentioned social networks and web based companies. It's equally relevant to other organizations in the Medicine, Universities, Finance, Healthcare, Government, sales and retail, and other industries. Big Data" not only implies many data, but more importantly, complicated data (Contributor, 2012). Personal user information, geo location, user-generated content, social graphs and machine logging are just a few examples of areas and applications in which the amount of data has been increasing exponentially.

There is nothing wrong with RDBMS but the needs of people are changing day by day. It is the procession of big data where SQL databases fail and NoSQL databases came into being. RDBMSs fail to handle big data. What actually Big Data is?

Big Data is actually the growth of data in an exponential manner. In 2001, an analyst Doug Laney introduced the concept of 3Vs in a research publication 3D data management. The concept revolves around 3Vs i-e data volume, variety and velocity and these 3Vs are important properties of big data. Volume denotes to the quantity of data, variety talks about the types of data and velocity refers to the speed require to process data. According to the model of 3Vs, the challenges of big data management depend on the growth of 3Vs, rather than just the volume alone (Whatis.techtarget.com, 2014).

3.5.   NoSQL Databases

In 1998, Carlo Strozzi used the term NoSQL to name his lightweight open-source RDBMS that used to store all data in the form of ASCII files and then made shell scripts as an alternative to SQL to access data (Vasiliev, 2013). In 2009, NoSQL started emerging when Johan Oskarsson arranged a meeting to discuss new technologies in IT industry about the storage and processing of data in San Francisco. In the same meeting, "NoSQL" word was put forward by Eric Evans. After that, Martin Fowler and Pramod J. Sadalage tried to consolidate knowledge about the NoSQL in his book "NoSQL Distilled"(Sadalage et. Al, 2013)

NoSQL stands for Not Only SQL. A NoSQL database is non-relational and as such just stores data without explicit and structured mechanisms to link different piles of data. NoSQL Databases are considered fast because data is usually denormalized. These types of non-relational databases are also called schema-less databases because they don't have proper models as we have in RDBMS (ERD) (w3resource, 2014).

NoSQL Databases have four main types described below:

3.5.1.   Key-Value Store

This type of NoSQL database allows storing key/value pairs and afterwards reading these values using the keys. The major advantage of using key-value store is having extremely efficient system during saving/reading values by keys because of the absence of the heavy layers of indexing systems, SQL handlers, profiling system evacuation etc, such solution offers the lowest cost of implementation, most efficient performance, and scaling (Vasiliev, 2013)

It uses JavaScript Object Notation (JSON) to represent data that separates the key/value pairs by a colon (Alex et. Al, n.d)

For example:

Key: 1   ID: abc; first Name: Sam

Key: 2   Email: alvina@gmail.com; Location: London; Age: 22

Key: 3   Facebook ID: userID;   Password: xxx; Name: Alvina

Some common key-value store databases are Amazon DynamoDB, Riak, Redis, LevelDB, Scalaris, MemcacheDB and Kyoto Cabinet (Edlich, 2014).

3.5.2.   Column Oriented

In column oriented databases, data is saved and retrieved by columns instead of rows just like RDBMS and peer to peer architecture is being followed in this type (Alex et. Al, n.d.).

Fundamentally, there are two dimensional arrays having one or more key/value pairs attached to it and hence allow very big data to be stored.

Some common column oriented databases are Hadoop/HBase, Accumulo, HPCC and Amazon SimpleDB (Edlich, 2014).

3.5.3. Document Based

Document-stored databases often offer great performance. Document oriented databases map each key with a complex data structure known as a document. Documents can contain many different key-value pairs, or key-array pairs, or even nested documents. (Mongodb.com, 2014)

Documents inside a document-oriented database are a bit similar to number of records in relational databases, but documents are much more flexible since they are unstructured and schema-less. The documents are stored in some standard format such as JSON, PDF, XML etc (Nayak et. Al., 2013). Each database is a collection of documents written in JSON format which is shown below:

{
Name: "Alvina Habib"
Age: 22
Contactno: 0777777777
Address: {
Houseno: 10
Street: xyz
Postcode: AL10 9BT
3
}}

MongoDB and CouchDB are the most popular Document based NoSQL databases.

3.5.4. Graph Based

Graph based databases use graph structures with nodes having edges and properties to store and retrieve data. This system also provides index-free adjacency i-e every element contains a direct pointer to its neighboring element and index.

Graph based database is shown in the Figure 4 below:

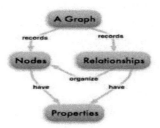

Figure 4: Graph Based NoSQL Databases

Some popular examples of Graph Based databases are AllegroGraph, InfoGrid, and Neo4j.

In Figure 5 below, all NoSQL database types have been compared in terms of size and complexity (Alex et. Al, n.d):

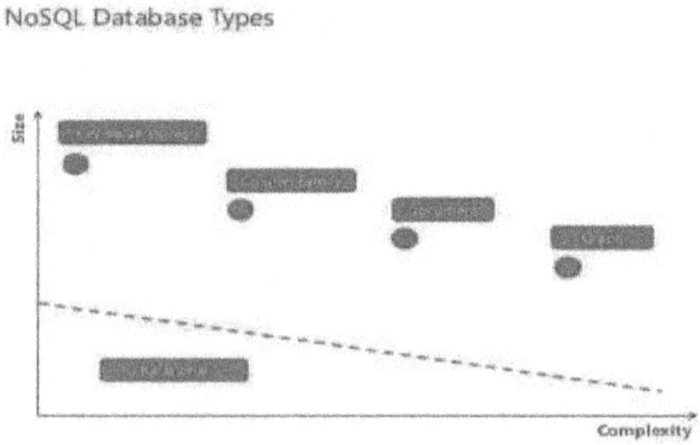

NoSQL Database Types

Figure 5: NoSQL Database Types

3.6.   Differences when moving from RDBMS to NoSQL

When moving from Relational DBMSs world to NoSQL world, obviously things do differ enormously. This section of my report gives readership an outlook on what are the major and minor differences when people move from RDBMS to NoSQL solution.(SÖDERGREN et. Al, 2011)

3.6.1. ACID and BASE

There are two main types of data transactions:

3.6.1.1 ACID

ACID is an abbreviation of **A**tomicity, **C**onsistency, **I**solation and **D**urability. ACID properties make sure the reliability of the database system.

Atomicity states that database's transactional variations must follow an "**All or nothing**" rule which means all parts of the transaction should be completed. If one part fails, the whole transaction fails (Chapple, 2014). In NoSQL, **Atomicity** of the transactions differs from one database type to another. For example, when using key-value stores type of NoSQL database, it varies from one solution to another. Atomicity is usually supportive for a single key, but multiple keys' functionality depends on the provider like Amazon S3 offers full atomicity over multiple keys [10] whereas Google App Engine simply deals with single key (SÖDERGREN et. Al, 2011).

Consistency describes that transaction will be valid only and the database should always be in consistent state before and after transaction. If some parts of transaction violate the database's consistency rules after execution, then whole transaction will be rolled back and the database will be restored to a state it was in before transaction by fulfilling those rules (Chapple, 2014). There are two types of database consistency i-e Strong consistency and eventual consistency. Strong consistency imposes that the database is always in consistent state whereas eventual consistency possess a time slot where the database is inconsistent but as the modification is replicated across, the servers and the whole database system eventually becomes consistent.

When it comes to consistency in NoSQL, the solutions differ depending on their position in the CAP triangle which will be discussed later in this report. The document-oriented databases' solutions vary as well. MongoDB only offers eventual consistency while CouchDB offers strong consistency but only for master-slave replication. Nothing general can be said about graph databases either but neo4j implements strong consistency (SÖDERGREN et. Al, 2011)

Isolation ensures that concurrent transactions will not impact each other's execution and no two transactions can overlap (Chapple, 2014). Isolation is very difficult to deal with and to implement in RDBMS's. Standard RDBMSs use the read and write locks, logs, rollbacks and deadlock detection to confirm this property. This procedure is quite different and results in many exceptions. However, NoSQL solutions deal with the problems of isolation in a well-organized way. The typical method of ensuring isolation is very expensive and does not favor speed or scalability. As an alternative, many NoSQL databases deal with other standard solutions. The first, cheap and most convenient one is to implement it for single key-value or a single document. However, if there is a need to implement isolation for bigger transactions, there is a requirement for another type of isolation and the solutions mostly used today are forms of Multiversion concurrency control (SÖDERGREN et. Al, 2011)

Durability confirms that transactions committed to the database will not be gone even if a crash occurs (Chapple, 2014). In RDBMS, normally this is done by maintaining a log file which is committed prior to the actual disk write. If the database crashes, the client rollbacks the committed transactions. Durability is quite easy process to implement but in case of distributed databases, the process differs where it means how durable the database is in the occurrence of devastation. Amazon claims that their S3 solution will still offer durability even if one of their main data centers gets damaged. Google App Engine provides customers to select from a highly replicating and more durable solution. Document-Oriented (both MongoDB and CouchDB) definitely support durability. MongoDB ensures this property using a log, called a journal and CouchDB always flushes its data to the disk and keeps older revisions. Neo4j as well supports typical durability (SÖDERGREN et. Al, 2011)

ACID properties can be implemented in distributed databases by using two-phase commit technique or by lacking but, it can result in temporary blockage of transactions so there are chances that a database may get an inconsistent state. However, NoSQL databases are not always in a consistent state as the transactions are mostly slow for modifications but resultantly the database gets consistent state after a while. Hence, NoSQL solutions are appropriate for applications where the database doesn't always need a consistent state and data is massive like Facebook, LinkedIn or twitter.

3.6.1.2 BASE

BASE is an abbreviation of **Bas**ic Availability, Soft State and Eventual Consistency. BASE is an alternative to ACID. Where ACID enforces database's consistency at the end of every operation, BASE accepts that the database consistency will be in a state of change. BASE ensures scalability that is very difficult to obtain with ACID properties (Pritchett, 2008)

3.6.2. CAP-Theorem

CAP theorem is also known as Brewer's theorem because Eric Brewer, a professor at the University of California, Berkeley, and CEO and scientist at Inktomi, made the assumption that Web services cannot guarantee all three of the following properties on one occasion (Pritchett, 2008):

Consistency: The client perceives that all set of operations has occurred at a time (Gilbert et. Al, 2012)

Availability: The second demand of the CAP-Theorem is the availability. Availability states that each sending request ultimately gets a response. Apparently, fast response is superior to slow response, but for the purpose of CAP, it justifies that even demanding an ultimate response is adequate to create a number of problems (Gilbert et. Al, 2012)

Partition tolerance: The third property of the CAP theorem is that the service should be partition tolerant (Gilbert et. Al, 2012)

Precisely, a Web service can support, maximum, only two of above mentioned properties with any database model or design. Designers and engineers are enforced to choose one between consistency and availability because any horizontal scaling approach is grounded on data partitioning (Pritchett, 2008).

The following figure provides a landscape of CAP-Theorem and a visual guide to NoSQL Systems (Hurst, 2014)

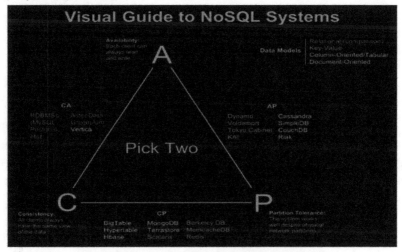

Figure 6: Visual Guide to NoSQL Systems

Standard RDBMSs are usually in consistent and available states while ensuring lower tolerance for network partitions. On the other hand, most NoSQL-solutions tend to compromise on either consistency or availability in order to achieve partition-tolerance (Gilbert et. Al, 2012) (Hurst, 2014)

3.6.3. Replication

With replication there is no need to spend excessive resources in order to prevent failures, but if failure of one of the nodes occurs, then there must be at least one other node that has the same data (replica) and can substitute the failed node. The disadvantage of using replication is if there is a need to write anything to the database, one has to write data to each and every node including replicas that is supposed to store that piece of data. It can be done in two ways master-slave strategy or master-master/multi-master strategy (SÖDERGREN et. Al, 2011)

3.6.4. Sharding

Sharding is used for the division of reads and writes over multiple servers. However sharding has some problems too. The first one is that databases' operations become very inefficient and complex using sharding. Normally these come in the form of the standard join procedures like relational DBMSs. This is the reason that joins are not supported in majority of sharded databases. The second disadvantage is that with the increasing number of nodes, there is higher probability of a node's failure. To cope up with this problem, designers combine sharding with replication (SÖDERGREN et. Al, 2011)

3.7.   Relational vs NoSQL Databases

In order to process huge amount of data there is a need to have flexible schemas as well as fast and efficient storage methods. NoSQL databases are claimed to fulfill these requirements. Moreover, NoSQL database are claimed to perform better in performance than relational databases but that performance varies with the type of operation (Li et. Al., 2013)

The key advantage of non-relational databases' approach is flexibility. One can insert or delete the corresponding columns without data loss. In contrast, such actions lead to loss of information in SQL databases. Moreover, with key/value storage methods, one can create more complex operations without having to make changes in the language of the application. It is also claimed that NoSQL is less expensive than SQL databases. Because NoSQL databases require more work from developer, but they are also very flexible and control the database performance. (Warden, 2011)

21

NoSQL databases have been claimed to outperform SQL databases because of the following advantages:

1) NoSQL databases allow agile reading and writing of data. (Han et al., 2011)

2) They allow for massive storage of data possible (Han et al., 2011)

3) Because they are schema-less, they are easy to scale (Nayak et Al., 2013)

4) They are open source and therefore there are no costs of hardware and/or licenses like a few relational databases. (Han et al., 2011)

5) At times, joins in SQL databases slow down the system but they work efficiently in NoSQL databases (Syoncloud.com, 2014)

6) NoSQL databases work efficiently when there is a need to analyze unstructured data such as the number of documents, some log files or semi-structured data such as CSV files and exports from other systems. (Syoncloud.com, 2014)

7) NoSQL databases aim for quick iteration and frequent code pushes because Object-oriented programming is easy and flexible to use with non-relational databases. (Mongodb.com, 2014)

8) There is no need for database administrators. (Nayak et al., 2013)

However, NoSQL have some drawbacks too:

1) They do not support SQL which is the industry standard (Han et al., 2011)

2) Document stores in a database should be avoided if the database has a lot of relations and normalization. (Nayak et Al., 2013)

3) Because NoSQL database products have been created only in recent years, they have not yet matured enough and hence lack transactions, reports and other additional features (Han et al., 2011)

4) NoSQL databases have a very narrow focus and therefore hardly perform other functionalities beyond their main focus (i-e to deal with of big data) (Greene, 2014)

5) Most designers and developers are at ease with RDBMS concepts and techniques. Therefore NoSQL database industry lacks in expertise (Technirvanaa.wordpress.com, 2011).

The comparison of relational and Document Based NoSQL database is shown in Figure 7 below: (McNulty, 2014)

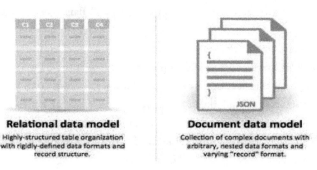

Relational data model

Highly-structured table organization
with rigidly-defined data formats and
record structure.

Document data model

Collection of complex documents with
arbitrary, nested data formats and
varying "record" format.

Figure 7: Relational Data Model vs Document Data Model

3.8.   Related Literature Work

(Roijackers, 2014) reviews the issues of permitting access in a uniform way.

According to (Meijer et Al., n.d), Microsoft provides a clear and theoretical framework that satisfies the idea we have about NoSQL databases.

(Bartholomew, 2010) has discussed the history of NoSQL and SQL databases as well as their differences.

(Sakr et al., 2011) included NoSQL in a discussion of data management solutions for cloud-based platforms.

(Varley, 2009) thoroughly discusses benefits, detriments, design strategies and a survey of available non-relational databases.

Some view NoSQL as a hype and state that the problems NoSQL claims to solve are not produced by the relational structure of SQL databases (Stonebraker, 2010)

(Cattell, 2011) has compared both SQL and different categories of NoSQL databases.

(Cooper et al., 2010) reported the performance results for four database systems compared to the YCSB benchmark.

After discussing with my supervisor, the following case study was put forward for research on comparison of performances of three databases. This case study has been taken from the text book "Fundamentals of Database Systems by Elmasri 6th Edition" (Elmasri, 2011) and this case study has been explained comprehensively at (Academic2.strose.edu, 2014) and (LBS kuttipedia, 2013)

The case study is about Airline Information System that represents each AIRPORT that keeps record of its unique Airport_ID, the AIRPORT_Name and the location of the AIRPORT (City and State).

Information on AIRPLANEs and AIRPLANE_TYPEs are also kept. For each AIRPLANE_TYPE (e.g, DS-12), the Type_Name, the manufacturing Company, and Maximum Number of Seats are kept. For each AIRPLANE, the Airplane_ID, Total_Seats, and TYPE are saved.

Each FLIGHT has a unique Flight_Number, the Airline for the FLIGHT and the Scheduled Weekdays of FLIGHT (e.g, every day of the week except Sunday).

Each FLIGHT has one or more FLIGHT_LEGs. Flight_Leg is a Segment of a flight containing a stopover, change of Airplane or change of Airline from one landing point to another (e.g, Flight_Number CO1023 from Las Vegas to Los Angeles can have two FLIGHT LEGs: Leg_Number 1 from Las Vegas to New York and Leg_Number 2 from New York to Los Angeles).. Each FLIGHT_LEG has a DEPARTURE_AIRPORT and Scheduled_Departure_Time and an ARRIVAL_AIRPORT and Scheduled_Arrival_Time.

A LEG INSTANCE is an instance of a FLIGHT_LEG on a particular Date (e.g, CO1223 Leg_Number 1 on June 08, 1992). The actual Departure and Arrival AIRPORTs and their departure and arrival times are kept for each Flight_Leg after the Flight_Leg has been concluded. The Num_of_Avail_Seats and the AIRPLANE used in the LEG_INSTANCE are also recorded. There are Leg Instances that may be different than planned Flight_Leg (s). Each Leg instance must have an associated Leg Instance; however, it also has the associated unique date as well as the record of available seats. Each Leg Instance arrives at some associated (at most one) airport and departs from (at most one) associated airport at certain times.

Each Leg Instance has a corresponding (at most one) Airplane assigned. There are Seats that are reserved on Leg Instances. Each Seat has a unique Seat No, and must belong to a Leg Instance (at most one).

The customer RESERVATIONs on each LEG INSTANCE includes the Customer Name, Phone, and Seat Number(s) for each reservation".

5.1.   Design, Modelling and Implementation in PostgreSQL and SQL

In order to design case study "Airline Information System" in PostgreSQL and SQL Databases, first of all I made logical model i-e ERD i-e the logical model of the entities, attributes and the relationships between entities with each other. The logical model (ERD) has been taken from (Elmasri, 2011) and shown in Figure 8 below:

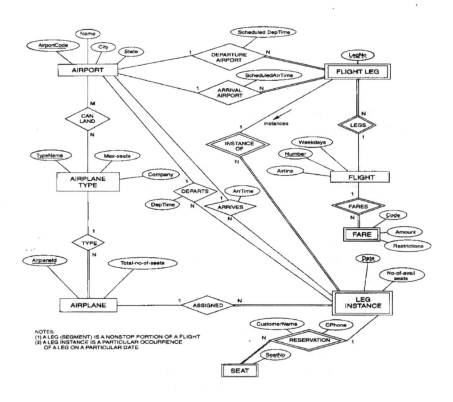

Figure 8: Logical Model of Airline Information System

After designing the logical model (ERD), I mapped the ER diagram of this case study into the tables. I have done ER to relational mapping in the following procedure:

ER to Relational Mapping:

Entities:

Airline Information System has eight main entities (tables/relations) i-e (Airplane, Airplane_Type, Airport, Fare, Flight, Flight_Leg, Leg_Instance, and Seat_Reservations) and one link table (Can_Land).

Attributes:

Entity 1: Airport

Airport has four attributes i-e Airport_ID, Name, City and state. Airport_ID is unique so it is the primary key of this entity.

Entity 2: Airplane_Type

Airplane_Type has three attributes i-e Type_Name, Max_Seats and the Company. Type_Name is unique so it is the primary key of this entity.

Entity 3: Airplane

Airplane has two attributes i-e Airplane_ID and Total_Seats. Airplane_ID is unique so it is the primary key of this entity.

Entity 4: Flight

Flight has three attributes i-e Flight_Number, Weekdays and Airline. Flight_Number is unique so it is the primary key of this entity.

Entity 5: Fare

Fare has three attributes i-e Code, Amount and Restrictions. Code is unique so it is the primary key of this entity.

Entity 6: Flight_Leg

Flight_Leg has three attributes i-e Leg_Number, Sch_Departure_Time and Sch_Arrival_Time. Leg_Number is unique so it is the primary key of this entity.

Entity 7: Leg_Instance

Leg_Instance has four attributes i-e Date, Num_of_Avail_Seats, Dep_Time and Arr_Time. Date is unique so it is the primary key of this entity.

Entity 8: Seat_Reservations

Seat_Reservations has three attributes i-e Seat_Number, Customer_Name and Cphone. Seat_Number is unique so it is the primary key of this entity.

Representation of Relationships:

One to Many:

In this case study, there are seven following One-to-Many relationships:

Airplane_Type: Airplane (1: M)

Airplane: Leg_Instance (1: M)

Leg_Instance: Seat_Reservations (1: M)

Flight: Fare (1: M)

Flight: Flight_Leg (1: M)

Airport: Flight_Leg (1: M)

Flight_Leg: Leg_Instance (1: M)

Airport: Leg_Instance (1: M)

In case of 1: M relationships, we have to put the primary key of the parent relation into the child relation where it becomes foreign key represented by a (*) in the following tables. By doing so, I got the following results:

Airport (Airport_ID, Name, City, State)

AirplaneType (Type_Name, Max_Seats, Company)

Airplane (Airplane_ID, Total_Seats, Type_Name*)

Flight (Flight_Number, Weekdays, Airline)

Fare (Flight_Number*, Code, Amount, Restrictions)

Flight_Leg (Flight_Number*, Leg_Number, Sch_Departure_Airport_ID*, Sch_Departure_Time, Sch_Arrival_Airport_ID*, Sch_Arrival_Time)

Leg_Instance (Date, Leg_Number*, Flight_Number*, Num_of_Avail_Seats, Airplane_ID*, Actual_Dep_Airport_ID*, Dep_Time, Actual_Arriv_Airport_ID*, Arr_Time)

Seat_Reservations (Seat_Number, Date*, Leg_Number*, Flight_Number*, Customer_Name, Cphone)

Many to Many:

In this case study, there is only 1 Many to Many relationship which is as follows:

Airport: Airplane_Type (M: N)

In this case, we need to introduce a third Link relation and copy primary keys from original two relations into that table. By doing so I got the following results:

Can_Land (Airport_ID*, Type_Name*)

Putting all the above results together, I got nine mapped tables (Airplane, Airplane_Type, Airport, Can_Land, Fare, Flight, Flight_Leg, Leg_Instance, and Seat_Reservations) along with their attributes and keys (primary, composite and foreign). The results are shown below:

Airport (Airport_ID, Name, City, State)

Airplane_Type (Type_Name, Max_Seats, Company)

Airplane (Airplane_ID, Total_Seats, Type_Name*)

Flight (Flight_Number, Weekdays, Airline)

Fare (Flight_Number*, Code, Amount, Restrictions)

Can_Land (Airport_ID*, Type_Name*)

Flight_Leg (Flight_Number*, Leg_Number, Sch_Departure_Airport_ID*, Sch_Departure_Time, Sch_Arrival_Airport_ID*, Sch_Arrival_Time)

Leg_Instance (Date, Leg_Number*, Flight_Number*, Num_of_Avail_Seats, Airplane_ID*, Actual_Dep_Airport_ID*, Dep_Time, Actual_Arriv_Airport_ID*, Arr_Time)

Seat_Reservations (Seat_Number, Date*, Leg_Number*, Flight_Number*, Customer_Name, Cphone)

After mapping into tables, I made physical model of mapped tables using Aqua Data Studio tool (Aquafold.com, 2014). The physical model is shown in Figure 9 below:

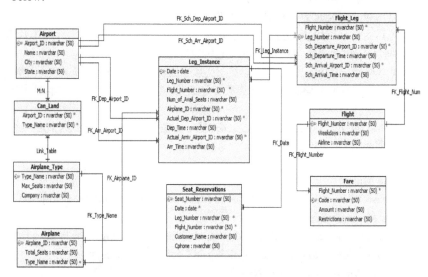

Figure 9: Physical Model of Airline Information System

Third step is to insert data into these mapped tables. For this purpose, in order to work in PostgreSQL server I installed pgAdmin III (Pgadmin.org, 2014) in windows 7 and to work in SQL I installed SQL Server 2008 along with SQL SERVER MANAGEMENT STUDIO 2008. In both database servers, I created three databases:

1) with no records; 2) a database consisting of five records 3) and a database consisting of 10 records.

I collected data from different sources (Aircraft-registration-country-codes.blogspot.co.uk, 2014), (Airlinecodes.co.uk, 2014) and (Flightradar24.com, 2014) and inserted them into above mentioned nine tables.

5.2. MongoDB

MongoDB is document-oriented NoSQL Database that is highly scalable with high-performance. It is an open source database written in C++ used by many companies all over the world, across all industries and for wide-ranging applications. MongoDB is an agile solution that allows database schemas to vary rapidly with the evolution of applications and still provides the functionalities designers and engineers expect from RDBMSs like a full query language, secondary indexing and strict consistency (Mongodb.com, 2014) (SÖDERGREN et. Al, 2011)

In the Figure 10 below, there is a comparison of RDBMS and MongoDB terms/concepts (Aruizca.com, 2014):

SQL Terms/Concepts	MongoDB Terms/Concepts
database	database
table	collection
row	document or BSON document
column	field
index	index
table joins	embedded documents and linking
primary key	primary key
Specify any unique column or column combination as primary key.	In MongoDB, the primary key is automatically set to the _id field.
aggregation (e.g. group by)	aggregation framework

Figure 10: SQL Terms/Concepts vs NoSQL Terms/Concepts

MongoDB has collections like RDBMSs have tables/relations. Inside each collection there are one or more documents and each document is JavaScript Object Notation (JSON) like data structure which is composed of field-value pairs, the document structure is as follows:

{

Field1: "Value1",

30

Field2: "Value2",

Field3: "Value3",

....

FieldN: "ValueN"

}

JavaScript Object Notation (JSON) is human-readable, plain text format to express structured data with support in many programming languages (Mongodb.com, 2014)

5.2.1. Features of MongoDB

Some features of MongoDB are explained below (Mongodb.org, 2014) (SÖDERGREN et. Al, 2011):

Document-Oriented Storage:

MongoDB is document oriented database and the insertion of data is in form of JSON documents that map programming language data types in a well-organized way. Embedded data models and arrays minimize the need of complex join operations as we do in RDBMSs. MongoDB is Dynamic and flexible because it does not have any fixed schema (schema-less).

Replication & High Availability:

MongoDB offers the use of Master-slave replication. Replication process has already been explained in section 3.6.3 of this report.

High Performance:

Use of embedding instead of complex join operations makes database reads and writes fast. Indexes include indexing of keys from embedded documents and arrays.

Auto-Sharding:

MongoDB support horizontal scaling without compromising functionality. Sharding process has already been explained in section 3.6.4 of this report.

Map/Reduce Views and Indexes:

MongoDB consumes Google's Map/Reduce strategies to generate views i-e a procedure of aggregating and reporting on the documents in the database. They are built dynamically and one can have as many different views of the same data as they want.

31

5.2.2. Data Models of MongoDB

Unlike relational databases where one has to have a schema in the form of tables/relations before insertion of data, MongoDB supports flexible schemas. Collections of MongoDB do not impose document structure. This flexibility of schema assists the fast mapping of documents to an entity/object. Each document inside the collection can match the data fields of the represented entity, even if the data varies substantially (Mongodb.org, 2014)

In order to design schema in MongoDB, there are two ways that allow databases to represent the relationships between collections which are discussed below:

5.2.2.1 References

Referencing is one way to represent the relationships between data collections by including links/references from one document to another inside. Applications can access the related data by resolving these references. Mostly, references are normalized data models.

Consider the Figure 11 below that represents referencing data model to link user, contact and access documents. Both the contact and access documents have a reference to the user document (Mongodb.org, 2014).

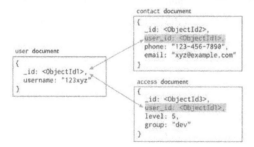

Figure 11: Referencing Data Model

5.2.2.2 Embedded Data

Embedded documents represent relationships between data by storing related data in single nested document structure. MongoDB documents support to embed document structures as nested documents or having array within a document. These are denormalized data models that allow applications to access and manipulate related

32

data in a single database procedure. The structure for embedding data is presented in Figure 12 (Mongodb.org, 2014)

```
{
    _id: <ObjectId1>,
    username: "123xyz",
    contact: {
            phone: "123-456-7890",        Embedded sub-
            email: "xyz@example.com"      document
          },
    access: {
            level: 5,                      Embedded sub-
            group: "dev"                   document
          }
}
```

Figure 12: Embedding Data Model

5.2.3. Design, modelling and Implementation of Airline Information System in MongoDB

In order to design, model and implement Airline Information System in MongoDB, first of all I designed my own schema and presented it to my supervisor Rene, just to give readership a rough idea how I modelled my collections. I used both embedding and referencing strategies to model the relationships between collections and documents. The self-designed schema is shown in figure below:

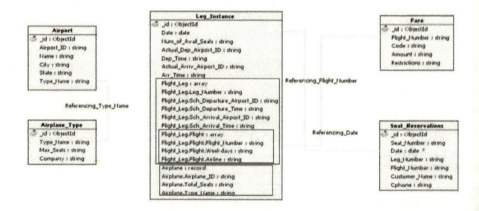

Figure 13: Self-Designed Schema for MongoDB

33

Collections:

I created five collections (Airport, Airplane_Type, Leg_Instance, Fare and Seat_Reservations) in using Robomongo 0.8.3 tool for MongoDB.

Relationships:

In order to represent relationship between collections and documents in MongoDB, embedding and referencing approaches are used. There are following three kinds of relationships in database systems and let's see below how to implement them in MongoDB:

One to One

There is no one-to-one relationship in this case study, but it is recommended to use embedding while implementing this type of relationship.

One to Many

There are following one-to-many relationships between collections in Airline Information System's case study:

Leg_Instance and Airplane

Leg_Instance and Airport

Flight_Leg and Leg_Instance

Flight and Flight_Leg

Flight and Fare

Leg_Instance and Seat_Reservations

Airport and Flight Leg

In order to implement one-to-many relationships, it is recommended to use embedding.

Embedding:

Using embedding data model, I embedded "Flight" collection inside "Flight_Leg", "Flight_Leg" inside "Leg_Instance" and "Airport" inside the "Leg_Instance". One has to embed one-side (Flight_Leg) inside many-side (Leg_Instance) while implementing one-to-many relationships. MongoDB is flexible because schemas can vary according to the needs of data retrieval. I embedded the above mentioned documents in order to extract the results of my query 4 that was implemented using Joins in PostgreSQL and SQL. The embedded documents are shown in Figure 14 below:

34

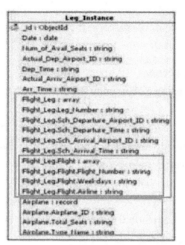

Figure 14: Embedded Documents

In order to insert one record of data in the embedded documents inside the collection "Leg_Instance" as shown in Figure 14 above, the format is as follows:

```
db.Leg_Instance.insert (
{
"_id" : ObjectId("53f4334d082f4b1f38e6d7cf"),
"Date" : ISODate("2012-02-09T00:00:00Z"),
"Leg_Number" : "1A",
"Flight_Number" : "5B/EAK",
"Num_of_Avail_Seats" : "11",
"Airplane_ID" : "14Z",
"Actual_Dep_Airport_ID" : "ADL",
"Dep_Time" : "1:10",
"Actual_Arriv_Airport_ID" : "ADL",
"Arr_Time" : "5:10",
"Flight_Leg":[{
"Flight_Number" : "5B/EAK",
"Leg_Number" : "1A",
"Sch_Departure_Airport_ID" : "ADL",
"Sch_Departure_Time" : "1:00",
"Sch_Arrival_Airport_ID" : "ADL",
"Sch_Arrival_Time" : "5:00",
```

```
"Flight":[{
"Flight_Number" : "5B/EAK",
"Weekdays" : "All Days",
"Airline" : "ATA Airlines",
}]
}],
"Airline":{"_id" : ObjectId("53f4334d082f4b1f38e6d7bb"),
"Airplane_ID" : "14Z",
"Total_Seats" : "150",
"Type_Name" : "Amazon",
}


})
```

From the above format, it can be seen that when I need to embed one document inside another I need to use array [] e.g when I embedded "Flight" inside "Flight_Leg", the format would be

```
"Flight":[{
  "Flight_Number" : "5B/EAK",
  "Weekdays" : "All Days",
  "Airline" : "ATA Airlines"
    }]
```

Many to Many
In relational databases, there is a need to create a link table to represent many to many relationships but in MongoDB referencing approach is used i-e one table has the reference from another table. In this case study, there is one many-to-many relationship between "Airport" and "Airplane_Type". It can be seen in Figure 14 below that "Airport" collection has "Type_Name" as reference from "Airplane_Type" collection

Referencing:
Referencing is another way to link documents and collection. In Figure 15 below, I referenced "Airport" to "Airplane_Type" by putting "Type_Name" as reference from "Airplane_Type" to "Airport".

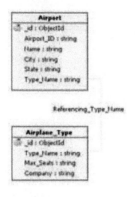

Figure 15: Referenced Documents

In order to insert one record in the above referenced collections, I used the following format:

db.Airport.insert (

{

"_id" : ObjectId("53f4334d082f4b1f38e6d7a7"),

"Airport_ID" : "ADL",

"Name" : "Abu Dhabi",

"City" : "Abu Dhabi",

"State" : "United Arab Emirates",

"**Type_Name**" : "Amazon",

})

In a similar way, "Fare" has reference of "Flight_Number" from "Flight" and "Seat_Reservations" has reference of "Date" from "Leg_Instance" shown in Figure 16 below:

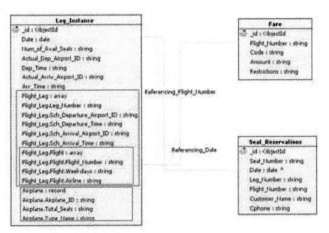

Figure 16: Embedded and Referenced Documents

In the above figure, it can be seen that "Seat_Reservations" has "Date" as reference from "Leg_Instance" and "Fare" has "Flight_Number" as reference from "Leg_Instance. Flight_Leg. Flight".

In order to insert one record in the above referenced collection "Seat_Reservations", I used the following format:

```
{
    "_id" : ObjectId("5411cfe11241f65b77151229"),
    "Seat_Number" : "09L",
    "Date" : "[2012/02/09]",
    "Leg_Number" : "1A",
    "Flight_Number" : "5B/EAK",
    "Customer_Name" : "Austen Wernick",
    "Cphone" : "4479460018"
}
```

Similarly, in order to insert one record in the above referenced collection "Fare", I used the following format:

```
{
    "_id" : ObjectId("5411cf811241f65b771511f9"),
    "Flight_Number" : "5B/EAK",
    "Code" : "00J",
    "Amount" : "200",
    "Restrictions" : "Alcohol"
}
```

38

6.1. Order of Complexity

I have given rank numbers to the queries that reflect their complexity (i-e the query ranked as 5 order is the most complex and the query with rank number 1 is the least complex.

Queries	Rank Order
1	3
2	4
3	1
4	5
5	2

Table 1: Ranks of queries in terms of complexity

Next, I wrote five different queries in PostgreSQL, SQL and NoSQL Databases and they are given below:

6.2. Query 1

Produce a list of all the companies names starting with A or B.

6.2.1. PostgreSQL

Select * from "Airplane_Type" where "Company" Like 'A%' or "Company" Like 'B%' Group By "Type_Name" Order By "Type_Name";

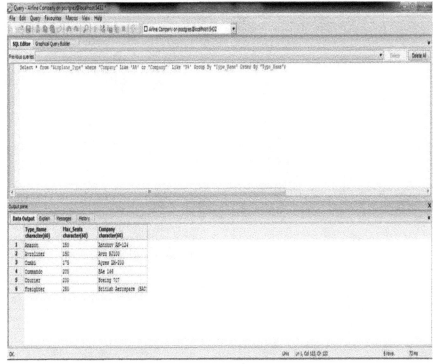

Figure 17: PostgreSQL Database's Query 1 Results

6.2.2. SQL

Select * from Airplane_Type where Company Like 'A%' or Company Like 'B%' Order By Type_Name;

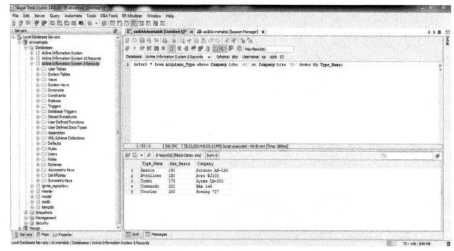

Figure 18: SQL Database's Query 1 Results

6.2.3. MongoDB

db.Airplane_Type.find ({$or: [{Company: /^A/}, {Company: /^B/}]}).sort ({"Type_Name": 1});

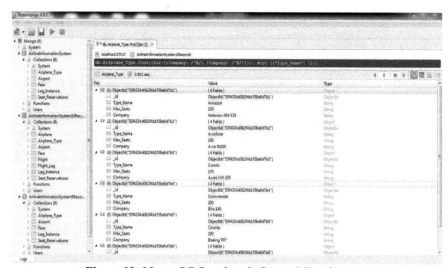

Figure 19: MongoDB Database's Query 1 Results

41

6.3. Query 2

Which airplane flew on Flight number BA/BAW leg number 3 on 2013-02-03?

6.3.1. PostgreSQL

Select "Airplane_ID" from "Leg_Instance" where "Flight_Number"='BA/BAW' and "Leg_Number"='3' and "Date"='2013-02-03' Group By "Airplane_ID" Order By "Airplane_ID";

Figure 20: PostgreSQL Database's Query 2 Results

6.3.2. SQL

Select Airplane_ID from Leg_Instance where Flight_Number='BA/BAW' and Leg_Number='1E' and Date='3/3/2013' Group By Airplane_ID Order By Airplane_ID;

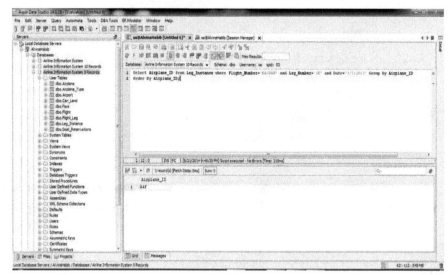

Figure 21: SQL Database's Query 2 Results

6.3.3. MongoDB

db.Leg_Instance.find ({"Date": {"$in" : [ISODate("2013-03-03T00:00:00.000Z")]},"Flight_Leg.Flight.Flight_Number": "BA/BAW", "Flight_Leg.Leg_Number": "1E",}, {"Airplane.Airplane_ID": 1}).sort ({"Airplane.Airplane_ID": 1});

Figure 22: MongoDB Database's Query 2 Results

43

6.4. Query 3

Find out the total reservations made in one year (from 2013-01-01 to 2014-01-01).

6.4.1. PostgreSQL

Select * from "Seat_Reservations" where "Date" between '2013-01-01' and '2014-01-01' Group By "Seat_Number" Order By "Seat_Number";

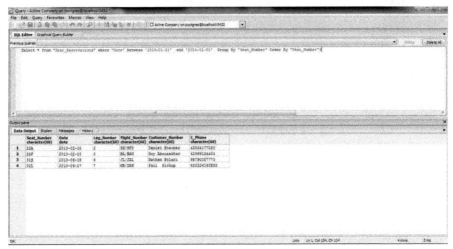

Figure 23: PostgreSQL Database's Query 3 Results

6.4.2. SQL

Select * from Seat_Reservations where Date between '2013-01-01' and '2014-01-01' Order By Seat_Number;

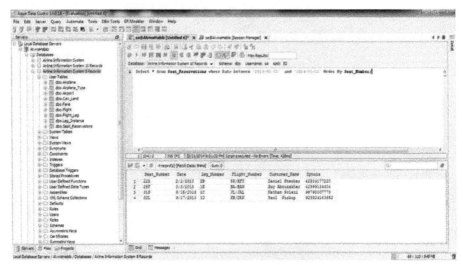

Figure 24: SQL Database's Query 3 Results

6.4.3. MongoDB

db.Seat_Reservations.find({ "Date" : { "$gte" : ISODate("2013-01-01T00:00:00.000Z") , "$lt" :ISODate("2014 01-01T00:00:00.000Z")}}).sort({"Seat_Number": 1});

Figure 25: MongoDB Database's Query 3 Results

45

6.5. Query 4

Show the airplane ID, airline and Num_of_Avail_Seats of Flight number is 'BA/BAW.

6.5.1. PostgreSQL

Select
"Flight"."Airline","Leg_Instance"."Num_of_Avail_Seats","Leg_Instance"."Airplane_I D","Leg_Instance"."Date" FROM public."Flight", public."Leg_Instance" WHERE "Flight"."Flight_Number"= "Leg_Instance"."Flight_Number" and
"Flight"."Flight_Number"='BA/BAW' Group By
"Flight"."Airline","Leg_Instance"."Num_of_Avail_Seats","Leg_Instance"."Airplane_I D","Leg_Instance"."Date" Order By
"Flight"."Airline","Leg_Instance"."Num_of_Avail_Seats","Leg_Instance"."Airplane_I D","Leg_Instance"."Date"

Figure 26: PostgreSQL Database's Query 4 Results

6.5.2. SQL

SELECT
Flight.Airline,Leg_Instance.Num_of_Avail_Seats,Leg_Instance.Airplane_ID,Leg_Inst ance.Date

46

FROM Flight,Leg_Instance WHERE Flight.Flight_Number =
Leg_Instance.Flight_Number and
   Flight.Flight_Number='BA/BAW'
   Group By
Flight.Airline,Leg_Instance.Num_of_Avail_Seats,Leg_Instance.Airplane_ID,
   Leg_Instance.Date Order By
Flight.Airline,Leg_Instance.Num_of_Avail_Seats,Leg_Instance.Airplane_ID,Leg_Inst
ance.Date;

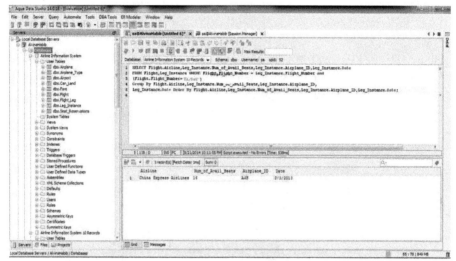

Figure 27: SQL Database's Query 4 Results

6.5.3. MongoDB

```
db.Leg_Instance.find({"Flight_Leg.Flight.Flight_Number":"BA/BAW"},
{"Flight_Leg.Flight.Airline":1, "Num_of_Avail_Seats": 1,
   "Airplane_ID": 1, "Date": 1}).sort({"Flight_Leg.Flight.Airline": 1,
   "Num_of_Avail_Seats": 1, "Airplane_ID": 1,"Date": 1
});
```

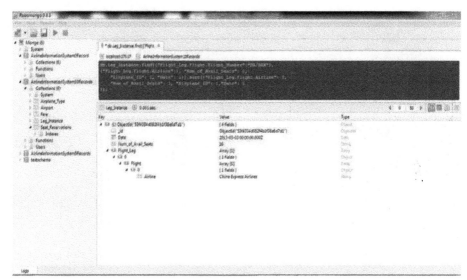

Figure 28: MongoDB Database's Query 4 Results

6.6. Query 5

Find out the airline types along with the names of their companies who have a Max_Seats>200.

6.6.1. PostgreSQL

Select * from "Airplane_Type" where "Max_Seats"> '200' Group By "Type_Name" Order By "Type_Name";

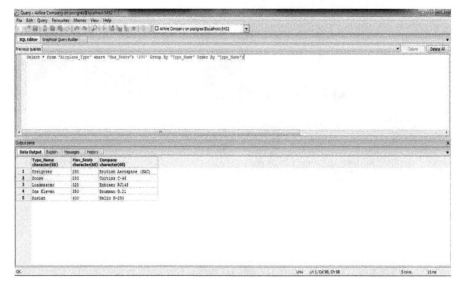

Figure 29: PostgreSQL Database's Query 5 Results

6.6.2. SQL

Select * from Airplane_Type where Max_Seats > '200' Order By Type_Name;

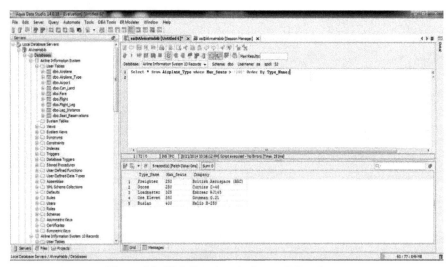

Figure 30: SQL Database's Query 5 Results

6.6.3. MongoDB

db.Airplane_Type.find({"Max_Seats": {"$gt": '200'}}).sort({"Type_Name": 1});

Figure 31: MongoDB Database's Query 5 Results

6.7. Runtime and Memory Usage Recordings

This was the most challenging part of my project because it was too difficult for me to find tools that measures memory used by queries at runtime because majority of the monitoring tools shows the memory utilization of exes' instead of queries.

For five repetitions of each query(five different queries in total) and for each of the three data base sizes (0, 5 and 10) I noted down the runtime and memory usage using different query tools in all three DBMSs. The results are listed in Appendices 1,2 and 3.

6.7.1. PostgreSQL

In PostgreSQL, I have used query tool in pgAdminIII. The run time taken by query 1 for five repetitions and for database size 10 is shown in Figure 32 below and runtimes have been highlighted with red box around them:

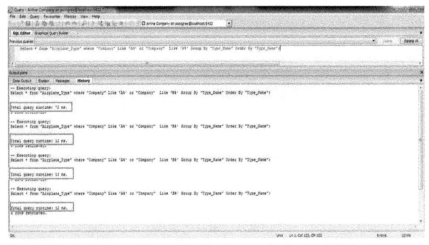

Figure 32: Run time taken by query 1 for 10 records (PostgreSQL Database).

Similarly, the memory usage of same query for database size 10 is highlighted and shown in Figure 33 below:

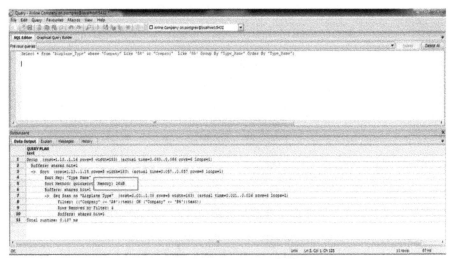

Figure 33: Memory used by query 1 for 10 records (PostgreSQL Database).

In a similar manner, I attained results for all other four queries for 5 repetitions.

For SQL, I used Aqua Data Studio (Aquafold.com, 2014) as a query tool and to measure queries' runtime and memory usages. The run time taken by query 1 for database size 10 is shown in Figure 34 below and runtime has been highlighted with red box around it:

Figure 34: Run time taken by query 1 for 10 records (SQL Database).

Similarly, the memory usage of same query for database size 10 is highlighted shown in Figure 35 below:

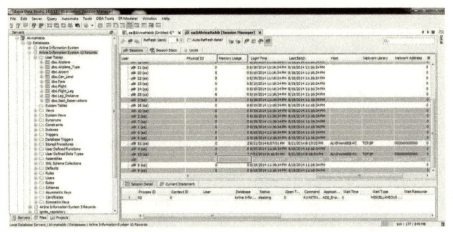

Figure 35: Memory used by query 1 for 10 records (SQL Database).

Queries' Memory usage for SQL Database has been measured using Aqua Data Studio. In the above figure it is visible that memory usage of process 52 is 3KB whereas process 52 is query execution's session.

In a similar manner, I attained results for all other four queries for 5 repetitions.

6.7.3. MongoDB

In MongoDB, I used Robomongo 0.8.3 as query tool. The run time taken by query 1 for database size 10 is highlighted with a red box and shown in Figure 36 below:

Figure 36: Run time taken by query 1 for 10 records (MongoDB Database).

From above figure it is clearly displayed that runtime of query 1 is 0.001 seconds, but for other two DBMSs I had runtime in milliseconds (ms). So, I converted sec to ms like 0.001/1000=1 ms.

Hence, the runtime for query 1 is 1 ms.

Similarly, the memory usage of same query for database size 10 is highlighted and shown in Figure 37 below:

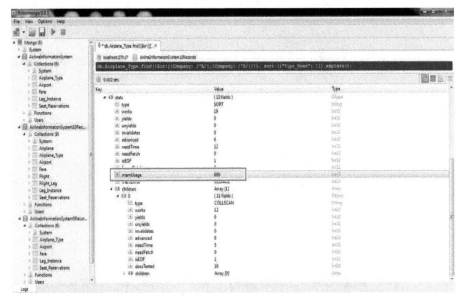

Figure 37: Memory used by query 1 for 10 records (MongoDB Database)

From above figure it is visible that memory usage of query 1 is 600 Int32, but for other two DBMSs I had memory usage in kilobytes (kb). So, I converted Int32 to Kb in the following way:

As 1 Int32=4Bytes

If we have 600Int32,

=>600 Int32=600*4

=2400Bytes

And 1 Byte=1000 Kilo Bytes

So, to get results in Kb

2400/1000=2.4Kb

Hence, the memory usage of query 1 in kilobytes (kb) is 2.4.

In a similar manner, I attained results for all other four queries for 5 repetitions.

This section has been the most interesting part of my investigation project. In this chapter, the statistical analysis has been carried out to find out the significant differences in performance (in terms of speed (runtime) and memory usage) w.r.t query type complexity and database size within each database and between three database systems i-e Object-Relational (PostgreSQL) DBMS, Relational (SQL) DBMS and Document-Oriented NoSQL (MongoDB) DBMS. This investigation is important because I have collected the data (queries' runtime and memory usage while execution) by using different tools for different database systems.

ANOVA

Analysis of Variance (ANOVA) is a statistical test use to test differences between two or more means of groups. By just looking at the collected data, one can probably see that there is a difference in runtime and memory usage between three above mentioned DBMSs to execute queries of varying complexities for varying databases sizes (0, 5 and 10), but the question is why I chose to apply statistical testing method analysis of variance ANOVA on my datasets?

The reason is that I was not just trying to figure out if there is a difference in performances within and between the group(s); I want to know if there is a statistically significant difference i-e real difference as defined by statistics.

There are three types of ANOVA.

Single-Factor or One-Way ANOVA:

Single-Factor ANOVA is performed to test variance among two or more independent groups of data, when the variance depends on a single factor. It is mostly applied when there are at least three groups of data.

Two-Factor or Two-Way ANOVA:

Two-way ANOVA is performed when the variance depends on two factors. There are two scenarios in which two-factor ANOVA can be applied (Controls.engin.umich.edu, 2014):

1. Two-Factor ANOVA without replication:

This type is performed when there is a need to collect a single data point for a specified condition.

2. Two-Factor ANOVA with replication:

This type is performed when there is a need to collect multiple data values for a specified condition (the total number of replicates must be specified and must be the same among different data groups)

I performed Two-Factor ANOVA with replication because there are number of replicates (multiple runs for each query statement).

There are many assumptions in two-factor ANOVA, one of them states that there should be no **significant outliers**. Outliers are values within data that follow the unusual pattern. The issue with outliers is that they can have a negative impact on the two-factor ANOVA, reducing the correctness of results. For this reason, I have replaced the outliers with their sample means in datasets. They are represented by bold or italic numbers in datasets.

If means are correlated to Standard Deviations of the groups, it means an underlying assumption of ANOVA is violated.

To avoid violation of this underlying assumption, I have taken logarithm of my datasets but there are some zero values in my data (for which log is undefined), so I have used the transformation $\ln(y+1)$ where y is the runtime (ms).

In order to test the difference in performance w.r.t Query type complexity and DB Size for each of the three Database systems i-e PostgreSQL, SQL and MongoDB Databases, I conducted two-way ANOVA but on the transformed data. Here, I have two Independent variables: X = Type of Query type complexity, this variable has c = 5 values ("levels") QS1 - QS5, Y= DB Size, this variable has c=3 values (0, 5 and 10) and 1 Dependent variable: Y = Run Time (ms)

In excel there is Data Analysis add on used to perform one-way and two-way ANOVA. Go to "Data Analysis" and select Anova: Two-Factor with Replication and define input and output ranges as shown in Figure 38 below:

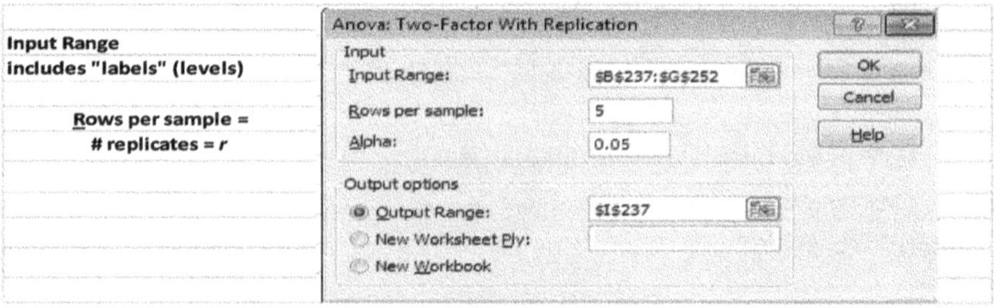

Figure 38: ANOVA in Excel

57

I have numbered the query statements Q1, Q2, Q3, Q4 and Q5 in correspondence to their complexity. Hence,

Was: Now:

$$Q1 \rightarrow Q3^*$$
$$Q2 \rightarrow Q4^*$$
$$Q3 \rightarrow Q1^*$$
$$Q4 \rightarrow Q5^*$$
$$Q5 \rightarrow Q2^*$$

Also, I have arranged the queries from low to high Q*, i.e. from left to right in the order Q1*, Q2*, Q3*, Q4* and Q5* in plots.

7.1.1. Two-Factor ANOVA w.r.t Database Size for each of the three Database Systems

First of all, in order to find out the variances in runtime w.r.t DB Size in performance, I applied two-**factor (Query Statement, DB Size)** ANOVA with replication on datasets of each of the three Database systems i-e PostgreSQL, SQL and MongoDB Databases.

For PostgreSQL Database

		QUERY STATEMENT				
		QS3	QS4	QS1	QS5	QS2
	0	1.176	1.146	1.079	1.114	1.114
		1.114	1.114	1.114	1.079	1.146
		1.146	1.146	1.114	1.176	1.146
		1.114	1.114	1.079	1.114	1.176
		1.079	1.079	1.176	1.114	1.114
	5	1.079	1.114	1.176	1.146	1.114
		1.146	1.114	1.146	1.146	1.146
DBSIZE		1.079	1.114	1.114	1.114	1.204
		1.114	1.176	1.176	0.699	1.079
		1.146	1.114	1.079	1.114	1.079
	10	1.146	1.114	1.114	1.146	1.079
		1.114	1.176	1.176	1.079	1.146
		1.146	1.146	1.114	1.079	1.146
		1.114	1.204	1.146	1.079	1.079
		1.114	1.114	0.778	1.146	1.079

Table 2: PostgreSQL Transformed Dataset

The Descriptive output below provides each group's sample size (r)/count, sum of groups, their mean/average, variance, degree of freedom (df) i-e count-1, sample standard deviation, the standard error of the mean (the standard deviation divided by the square root of r, which estimates the potential for sampling error and t value. Also, this part of the output presents the confidence interval within which we are 95% confident that the true population mean for this group would fall. The ANOVA results are given below, the averages and 95% confidence intervals of each group has been highlighted:

Anova: Two-Factor With Replication

SUMMARY		QS3	QS4	QS1	QS5	QS2	Total
	0						
sample size (r)	Count	5	5	5	5	5	25
	Sum	5.629287	5.599324	5.56234	5.597103	5.696234	28.08429
Sample mean (mj)	Average	1.125857	1.119865	1.112468	1.119421	1.139247	1.123372
Sample var (s2j)	Variance	0.001349	0.000776	0.001567	0.00123	0.000683	0.001019
	df = r - 1	4	4	4	4	4	24
	*Sample standard deviation (sj)	0.037	0.028	0.040	0.035	0.026	0.032
	*Standard Error (SEj = s/Vr)	0.016	0.012	0.018	0.016	0.012	0.006
	*t	2.776	2.776	2.776	2.776	2.776	2.064
	*95% Confidence Interval (Clj)	0.046	0.035	0.049	0.044	0.032	0.013
	5						
sample size (r)	Count	5	5	5	5	5	25
	Sum	5.564562	5.631865	5.691435	5.219113	5.622554	27.72953
Sample mean (mj)	Average	1.112912	1.126373	1.138287	1.043823	1.124511	1.109181
Sample var (s2j)	Variance	0.001121	0.000772	0.001751	0.037422	0.002757	0.008484
	df = r - 1	4	4	4	4	4	24
	*Sample standard deviation (sj)	0.033	0.028	0.042	0.193	0.053	0.092
	*Standard Error (SEj = s/Vr)	0.015	0.012	0.019	0.087	0.023	0.018
	*t	2.776	2.776	2.776	2.776	2.776	2.064
	*95% Confidence Interval (Clj)	0.042	0.035	0.052	0.240	0.065	0.038
	10						
sample size (r)	Count	5	5	5	5	5	25
	Sum	5.634086	5.754226	5.328257	5.5298	5.5298	27.77617
Sample mean (mj)	Average	1.126817	1.150845	1.065651	1.10596	1.10596	1.111047
Sample var (s2j)	Variance	0.000311	0.001555	0.026499	0.001345	0.001345	0.005998
	df = r - 1	4	4	4	4	4	24
	*Sample standard deviation (sj)	0.018	0.039	0.163	0.037	0.037	0.077
	*Standard Error (SEj = s/Vr)	0.008	0.018	0.073	0.016	0.016	0.015
	*t	2.776	2.776	2.776	2.776	2.776	2.064
	*95% Confidence Interval (Clj)	0.022	0.049	0.202	0.046	0.046	0.032
	Total						
sample size (r)	Count	15	15	15	15	15	
	Sum	16.82794	16.98541	16.58203	16.34602	16.84859	
Sample mean (mj)	Average	1.121862	1.132361	1.105469	1.089734	1.123239	
Sample var (s2j)	Variance	0.000838	0.001077	0.009488	0.012589	0.001566	
	df = r - 1	14	14	14	14	14	
	*Sample standard deviation (sj)	0.029	0.033	0.097	0.112	0.040	
	*Standard Error (SEj = s/Vr)	0.007	0.008	0.025	0.029	0.010	
	*t	2.145	2.145	2.145	2.145	2.145	
	*95% Confidence Interval (Clj)	0.016	0.018	0.054	0.062	0.022	

The ANOVA table is given below:

	ANOVA						
	Source of Variation	SS	df	MS	F	P-value	F crit
2nd factor (here:DBSize) →	Sample	0.002973	2	0.001486	0.277036	0.758992	3.150411
1st factor (here: Query Statements)→	Columns	0.017167	4	0.004292	0.799884	0.530043	2.525215
	Interaction	0.0329	8	0.004113	0.766465	0.633353	2.096968
	Within	0.321933	60	0.005366			
	Total	0.374974	74				

From above ANOVA Table, the five rows represent the variance between sample (here DB Size), between columns (here Query Statements), between interaction, Within Groups (query statements) and Total respectively. The first column provides us with the sum of squares for each variance group (query statement and DB Size) and its total. The second column represents the degrees of freedom between groups (r-1). The third column presents the Mean Square (MS) = SS/df. The fourth and fifth columns present the variance ratio i-e $Fstatistic = \dfrac{MS_{between}}{MS_{within}}$ and its associated level of significance (p-value) respectively. The last column gives us the value of F crit.

Take a look at the values of Fstatistic, Sig value (p-value) and F crit presented in the last three columns of ANOVA results in **above evaluation**. These values indicate if the conditions' means are statistically different. In this experiment, the p-values for sample, columns and interaction sources are 0.75, 0.53 and 0.63 respectively. Moreover consider the Fstatistic and Fcrit values, all of Fstatistics are < Fcrit, if Fstatistic<Fcrit and p-value>0.05, then I can conclude that the differences have not been found w.r.t DB Size using PostgreSQL Database System and they are not significant. I also conclude that the differences in runtimes are not likely due to change in DB Size using PostgreSQL Database. Also interaction is not significant in this case.

From the sample means, sample sizes, sample sum and variances, I have computed the standard deviations, sum of squares and standard error for each of the three DB Sizes. Then I multiplied the outcomes by the t-value for a significance level of 5% and the degrees of freedom for each sample (r − 1). This t-value has been found by using the Excel function "=TINV (0.05, df). The product is the 95% confidence interval. In order to find the 95% Confidence Intervals, I have taken the total of all query statements runtimes' average for each DB Size (0, 5 and 10). The bar plot of means of runtimes along with error bars for five query statements and DB Size (0, 5 and 10) using PostgreSQL Database is given below in figure 39 and figure 40 respectively:

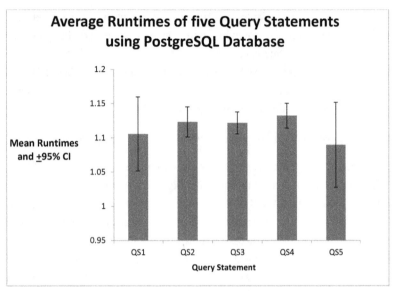

Figure 39: Plot of Five Queries' Runtime ±95% CI using PostgreSQL Database

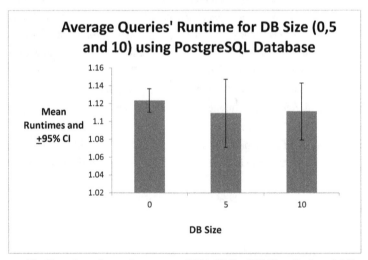

Figure 40: Bar plot of sample means ±95% CI for DB Size (0, 5 and 10) using PostgreSQL Database

Clearly, in figure, 39 and 40, the error bars are overlapping which means that the groups are not significant.

For SQL Database:

Just like PostgreSQL Database, I applied two-**factor (Query Statement, DB Size)** ANOVA with replication on SQL dataset to find out the variances in runtime w.r.t DB Size (0, 5 and 10) which is as follows:

		QUERY STATEMENT				
		QS3	QS4	QS1	QS5	QS2
	0	2.422	2.493	2.465	2.563	2.346
		2.396	2.320	2.243	2.314	2.250
		2.283	2.292	2.267	2.294	2.297
		2.314	2.270	2.294	2.334	2.281
		2.338	2.297	2.286	2.476	2.299
	5	2.588	2.484	2.428	2.537	2.299
		2.479	2.367	2.338	2.332	2.312
DBSIZE		2.401	2.270	2.281	2.384	2.294
		2.364	2.288	2.303	2.332	2.310
		2.340	2.486	2.288	2.418	2.452
	10	2.498	2.312	2.632	2.462	2.401
		2.449	2.415	2.322	2.452	2.286
		2.521	2.281	2.320	2.301	2.330
		2.407	2.267	2.288	2.324	2.336
		2.375	2.334	2.462	2.342	2.307

Table 3: SQL Transformed Dataset

Description has already been given above for PostgreSQL Database. The ANOVA results are given below and the averages and 95% confidence intervals of each group has been highlighted:

Anova: Two-Factor With Replication

	SUMMARY	QS3	QS4	QS1	QS5	QS2	Total
		0					
sample size (r)	Count	5	5	5	5	5	25
	Sum	11.75343	11.67134	11.55562	11.98194	11.47332	58.43565
Sample mean (mj)	Average	2.350686	2.334268	2.311123	2.396388	2.294665	2.337426
Sample var (s2j)	Variance	0.003287	0.008173	0.007824	0.01381	0.001209	0.007005
	df = r - 1	4	4	4	4	4	24
	*Sample standard deviation (sj)	0.057	0.090	0.088	0.118	0.035	0.084
	*Standard Error (SEj = s/vr)	0.026	0.040	0.040	0.053	0.016	0.017
	*t	2.776	2.776	2.776	2.776	2.776	2.064
	*95% Confidence Interval (CIj)	0.071	0.112	0.110	0.146	0.043	0.035
		5					
sample size (r)	Count	5	5	5	5	5	25
	Sum	12.17173	11.89469	11.63862	12.00355	11.66649	59.37509
Sample mean (mj)	Average	2.434347	2.378938	2.327724	2.40071	2.333298	2.375004
Sample var (s2j)	Variance	0.010096	0.010729	0.003643	0.007093	0.00444	0.007703
	df = r - 1	4	4	4	4	4	24
	*Sample standard deviation (sj)	0.100	0.104	0.060	0.084	0.067	0.088
	*Standard Error (SEj = s/vr)	0.045	0.046	0.027	0.038	0.030	0.018
	*t	2.776	2.776	2.776	2.776	2.776	2.064
	*95% Confidence Interval (CIj)	0.125	0.129	0.075	0.105	0.083	0.036
		10					
sample size (r)	Count	5	5	5	5	5	25
	Sum	12.24944	11.60939	12.02502	11.88192	11.66133	59.4271
Sample mean (mj)	Average	2.449889	2.321877	2.405005	2.376384	2.332265	2.377084
Sample var (s2j)	Variance	0.003737	0.003397	0.020705	0.005658	0.001899	0.008219
	df = r - 1	4	4	4	4	4	24
	*Sample standard deviation (sj)	0.061	0.058	0.144	0.075	0.044	0.091
	*Standard Error (SEj = s/vr)	0.027	0.026	0.064	0.034	0.019	0.018
	*t	2.776	2.776	2.776	2.776	2.776	2.064
	*95% Confidence Interval (CIj)	0.076	0.072	0.179	0.093	0.054	0.037
		Total					
sample size (r)	Count	15	15	15	15	15	
	Sum	36.17461	35.17542	35.21926	35.86741	34.80114	
Sample mean (mj)	Average	2.41164	2.345028	2.347951	2.391161	2.320076	
Sample var (s2j)	Variance	0.006925	0.007015	0.010985	0.007709	0.002503	
	df = r - 1	14	14	14	14	14	
	*Sample standard deviation (sj)	0.083	0.084	0.105	0.088	0.050	
	*Standard Error (SEj = s/vr)	0.021	0.022	0.027	0.023	0.013	
	*t	2.145	2.145	2.145	2.145	2.145	
	*95% Confidence Interval (CIj)	0.046	0.046	0.058	0.049	0.028	

The ANOVA table is given below:

	ANOVA						
	Source of Variation	SS	df	MS	F	P-value	F crit
2nd factor (here:DBSize) →	Sample	0.02491	2	0.012455	1.767508	0.179533	3.150411
1st factor (here: Query Statements)→	Columns	0.083261	4	0.020815	2.953944	0.027004	2.525215
	Interaction	0.044201	8	0.005525	0.784089	0.618368	2.096968
	Within	0.422793	60	0.007047			
	Total	0.575165	74				

Take a look at the values of Fstatistic, Sig value (p-value) and F crit presented in the last three columns of above ANOVA Table results. In this experiment, the p-values for sample, columns and interaction are 0.17, 0.02 and 0.61 respectively. Moreover, Fstatistic>Fcrit and also p-value < 0.05 only for Columns (Query Statements), I conclude that there is **no statistical significant difference in runtimes** w.r.t the DB Size but there is statistical significant difference w.r.t query type complexity using SQL Database. Moreover, the differences between runtimes are not likely due to

63

change in DB Size but they change due to Query Statements using SQL Database and interaction is not significant as well.

The plot of mean runtimes of five query statements +95% CI for DB Size (0, 5 and 10) using SQL Database is given below:

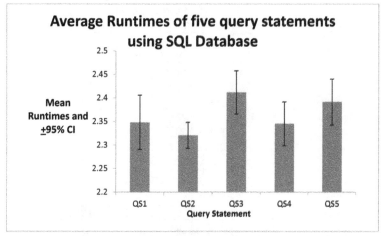

Figure 41: Bar plot of sample means ±95% CI using SQL Database

In figure 41, not all of the error bars are overlapping; it shows the significance of query type complexity using SQL Database.

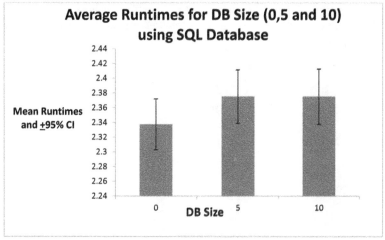

Figure 42: Bar plot of means ±95% CI for DB Size (0, 5 and 10) using SQL Database

For MongoDB Database

Just like PostgreSQL and SQL Databases, I applied two-**factor (Query Statement, DB Size)** ANOVA with replication on the dataset of MongoDB Database to find out the variances in runtime w.r.t DB Size (0, 5 and 10) which is as follows:

		QUERY STATEMENT				
		QS3	QS4	QS1	QS5	QS2
	0	0.398	0.439	0.301	0.477	0.477
		0.477	0.477	0.602	0.477	0.301
		0.301	0.477	0.477	0.477	0.301
		0.301	0.301	0.439	0.477	0.477
		0.477	0.477	0.301	0.301	0.477
	5	0.477	0.477	0.301	0.000	0.477
		0.301	0.301	0.477	0.477	0.602
DBSIZE		0.477	0.439	0.477	0.477	0.301
		0.301	0.477	0.477	0.301	0.699
		0.301	0.477	0.301	0.477	0.477
	10	0.301	0.352	0.477	0.477	0.301
		0.301	0.477	0.477	0.301	0.477
		0.477	0.301	0.477	0.477	0.602
		0.301	0.477	0.477	0.301	0.477
		0.477	0.000	0.301	0.301	0.301

Table 4: MongoDB Transformed Dataset

Description has already been given above for PostgreSQL Database. The ANOVA results are given below and the averages and 95% confidence intervals of each group has been highlighted:

	Anova: Two-Factor With Replication						
	SUMMARY	QS3	QS4	QS1	QS5	QS2	Total
	0						
sample size (r)	Count	5	5	5	5	5	25
	Sum	1.954243	2.171726	2.120574	2.209515	2.033424	10.48948
Sample mean (m_j)	Average	0.390849	0.434345	0.424115	0.441903	0.406685	0.419579
Sample var (s^2_j)	Variance	0.007768	0.005822	0.016251	0.006202	0.009302	0.007918
	df = r - 1	4	4	4	4	4	24
	*Sample standard deviation (sj)	0.088	0.076	0.127	0.079	0.096	0.089
	*Standard Error (SEj = s/vr)	0.039	0.034	0.057	0.035	0.043	0.018
	*t	2.776	2.776	2.776	2.776	2.776	2.064
	*95% Confidence Interval (CIj)	0.109	0.095	0.158	0.098	0.120	0.037
	5						
sample size (r)	Count	5	5	5	5	5	25
	Sum	1.857332	2.171726	2.033424	1.732394	2.556303	10.35118
Sample mean (mj)	Average	0.371466	0.434345	0.406685	0.346479	0.511261	0.414047
Sample var (s2j)	Variance	0.009302	0.005822	0.009302	0.043329	0.022502	0.018438
	df = r - 1	4	4	4	4	4	24
	*Sample standard deviation (sj)	0.096	0.076	0.096	0.208	0.150	0.136
	*Standard Error (SEj = s/vr)	0.043	0.034	0.043	0.093	0.067	0.027
	*t	2.776	2.776	2.776	2.776	2.776	2.064
	*95% Confidence Interval (CIj)	0.120	0.095	0.120	0.258	0.186	0.056
	10						
sample size (r)	Count	5	5	5	5	5	25
	Sum	1.857332	1.607455	2.209515	1.857332	2.158362	9.689998
Sample mean (mj)	Average	0.371466	0.321491	0.441903	0.371466	0.431672	0.3876
Sample var (s2j)	Variance	0.009302	0.03829	0.006202	0.009302	0.016825	0.015358
	df = r - 1	4	4	4	4	4	24
	*Sample standard deviation (sj)	0.096	0.196	0.079	0.096	0.130	0.124
	*Standard Error (SEj = s/vr)	0.043	0.088	0.035	0.043	0.058	0.025
	*t	2.776	2.776	2.776	2.776	2.776	2.064
	*95% Confidence Interval (CIj)	0.120	0.243	0.098	0.120	0.161	0.051
	Total						
sample size (r)	Count	15	15	15	15	15	
	Sum	5.669	5.951	6.364	5.799	6.748	
Sample mean (mj)	Average	0.378	0.397	0.424	0.387	0.450	
Sample var (s2j)	Variance	0.008	0.017	0.009	0.019	0.016	
	df = r - 1	14	14	14	14	14	
	*Sample standard deviation (sj)	0.087	0.132	0.096	0.136	0.127	
	*Standard Error (SEj = s/vr)	0.023	0.034	0.025	0.035	0.033	
	*t	2.145	2.145	2.145	2.145	2.145	
	*95% Confidence Interval (CIj)	0.048	0.073	0.053	0.075	0.070	

The ANOVA table is given below:

	ANOVA						
	Source of Variation	SS	df	MS	F	P-value	F crit
2nd factor (here:DBSize) →	Sample	0.014606	2	0.007303	0.508281	0.604095	3.150411
1st factor (here: Query Statements)→	Columns	0.05252	4	0.01313	0.913818	0.461853	2.525215
	Interaction	0.086511	8	0.010814	0.752625	0.64516	2.096968
	Within	0.862092	60	0.014368			
	Total	1.015729	74				

Take a look at the values of Fstatistic, Sig value (p-value) and F crit presented in the last three columns of ANOVA results in **Figure above**. In this case, the p-values for sample, columns and interaction are 0.60, 0.46 and0.64 respectively. Also F values are < Fcrit and also all Sig value> 0.05, I conclude that there is **no statistical significant difference in runtimes** w.r.t DB Size using MongoDB Database. I also conclude that the differences between runtimes are not likely due to change in DB Size using MongoDB Database and interaction is not significant as well.

The plot of means of mean runtime +95% CI using MongoDB Database is given below:

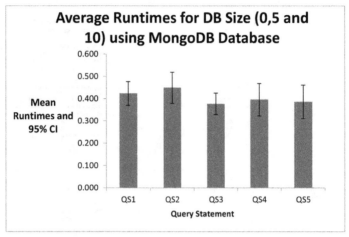

Figure 43: Bar plot of sample means ±95% CI using MongoDB Database

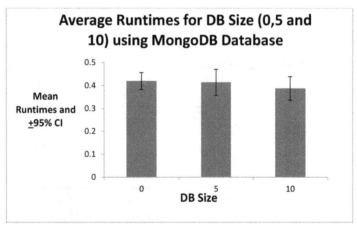

Figure 44: Bar Plot of sample means ±95% CI for DB Size (0, 5 and 10) using MongoDB Database

7.1.2 Two-Factor ANOVA to compare Queries' Runtime between three Database Systems

Now I want to find out if there is any statistical difference in runtime w.r.t Query type complexity irrespective of the DB Size (because I have already concluded above that DB Size doesn't affect the performance) between all three database systems (PostgreSQL, SQL and MongoDB) which are as follows:

		Query Statements				
		QS3	QS4	QS1	QS5	QS2
		1.176	1.146	1.079	1.114	1.114
		1.114	1.114	1.114	1.079	1.146
		1.146	1.146	1.114	1.176	1.146
		1.114	1.114	1.079	1.114	1.176
		1.079	1.079	1.176	1.114	1.114
		1.079	1.114	1.176	1.146	1.114
	PostgreSQL	1.146	1.114	1.146	1.146	1.146
		1.079	1.114	1.114	1.114	1.204
		1.114	1.176	1.176	0.699	1.079
		1.146	1.114	1.079	1.114	1.079
		1.146	1.114	1.114	1.146	1.079
		1.114	1.176	1.176	1.079	1.146
		1.146	1.146	1.114	1.079	1.146
		1.114	1.204	1.146	1.079	1.079
		1.114	1.114	0.778	1.146	1.079
		2.422	2.493	2.465	2.563	2.346
		2.396	2.320	2.243	2.314	2.250
		2.283	2.292	2.267	2.294	2.297
		2.314	2.270	2.294	2.334	2.281
		2.338	2.297	2.286	2.476	2.299
		2.588	2.484	2.428	2.537	2.299
Database Systems	SQL	2.479	2.367	2.338	2.332	2.312
		2.401	2.270	2.281	2.384	2.294
		2.364	2.288	2.303	2.332	2.310
		2.340	2.486	2.288	2.418	2.452
		2.498	2.312	2.632	2.462	2.401
		2.449	2.415	2.322	2.452	2.286
		2.521	2.281	2.320	2.301	2.330
		2.407	2.267	2.288	2.324	2.336
		2.375	2.334	2.462	2.342	2.307
		0.398	0.439	0.301	0.477	0.477
		0.477	0.477	0.602	0.477	0.301
		0.301	0.477	0.477	0.477	0.301
		0.301	0.301	0.439	0.477	0.477
		0.477	0.477	0.301	0.301	0.477
		0.477	0.477	0.301	0.000	0.477
	MongoDB	0.301	0.301	0.477	0.477	0.602
		0.477	0.439	0.477	0.477	0.301
		0.301	0.477	0.477	0.301	0.699
		0.301	0.477	0.301	0.477	0.477
		0.301	0.352	0.477	0.477	0.301
		0.301	0.477	0.477	0.301	0.477
		0.477	0.301	0.477	0.477	0.602
		0.301	0.477	0.477	0.301	0.477
		0.477	0.000	0.301	0.301	0.301

Table 5: Runtime Transformed Dataset for all three Databases

The Descriptive output has already been explained. The ANOVA results are given below and the averages and 95% confidence intervals of each group has been highlighted:

	SUMMARY	Q53	Q54	Q51	Q55	Q52	Total
	PostGreSQL						
sample size (r)	Count	15	15	15	15	15	75
	Sum	16.828	16.985	16.582	16.346	16.849	83.590
Sample mean (m_j)	Average	1.122	1.132	1.105	1.090	1.123	1.115
Sample var ($s^2{}_j$)	Variance	0.001	0.001	0.009	0.013	0.002	0.005
	df = r - 1	14	14	14	14	14	74
	*Sample standard deviation (s_j)	0.029	0.033	0.097	0.112	0.040	0.071
	*Standard Error ($SE_j = s/\sqrt{r}$)	0.007	0.008	0.025	0.029	0.010	0.008
	*t	2.145	2.145	2.145	2.145	2.145	1.993
	*95% Confidence Interval (CI_j)	0.016	0.018	0.054	0.062	0.022	0.016
	SQL						
sample size (r)	Count	15	15	15	15	15	75
	Sum	36.175	35.175	35.219	35.867	34.801	177.238
Sample mean (m_j)	Average	2.412	2.345	2.348	2.391	2.320	2.363
Sample var ($s^2{}_j$)	Variance	0.007	0.007	0.011	0.008	0.003	0.008
	df = r - 1	14	14	14	14	14	74
	*Sample standard deviation (s_j)	0.083	0.084	0.105	0.088	0.050	0.088
	*Standard Error ($SE_j = s/\sqrt{r}$)	0.021	0.022	0.027	0.023	0.013	0.010
	*t	2.145	2.145	2.145	2.145	2.145	1.993
	*95% Confidence Interval (CI_j)	0.046	0.046	0.058	0.049	0.028	0.020
	MongoDB						
sample size (r)	Count	15	15	15	15	15	75
	Sum	5.669	5.951	6.364	5.799	6.748	30.531
Sample mean (m_j)	Average	0.378	0.397	0.424	0.387	0.450	0.407
Sample var ($s^2{}_j$)	Variance	0.008	0.017	0.009	0.019	0.016	0.014
	df = r - 1	14	14	14	14	14	74
	*Sample standard deviation (s_j)	0.087	0.132	0.096	0.136	0.127	0.117
	*Standard Error ($SE_j = s/\sqrt{r}$)	0.023	0.034	0.025	0.035	0.033	0.014
	*t	2.145	2.145	2.145	2.145	2.145	1.993
	*95% Confidence Interval (CI_j)	0.048	0.073	0.053	0.075	0.070	0.027
	Total						*Total*
sample size (r)	Count	45	45	45	45	45	225
	Sum	58.671	58.112	58.165	58.013	58.398	
Sample mean (m_j)	Average	1.304	1.291	1.293	1.289	1.298	
Sample var ($s^2{}_j$)	Variance	0.727	0.668	0.658	0.718	0.618	
	df = r - 1	44	44	44	44	44	
	*Sample standard deviation (s_j)	0.852539	0.817333	0.811275	0.847126	0.786228	
	*Standard Error ($SE_j = s/\sqrt{r}$)	0.127089	0.121841	0.120938	0.126282	0.117204	
	*t	2.015368	2.015368	2.015368	2.015368	2.015368	
	*95% Confidence Interval (CI_j)	0.256131	0.245554	0.243734	0.254505	0.236209	

The ANOVA table is given below:

	ANOVA						
	Source of Variation	SS	df	MS	F	P-value	F crit
1st factor here (Database Systems) ->	Sample	147.148	2.000	73.574	8522.439	0.000	3.039
2nd Factor here (Query Statement) ->	Columns	0.006	4.000	0.002	0.180	0.949	2.415
	Interaction	0.147	8.000	0.018	2.125	0.035	1.983
	Within	1.813	210.000	0.009			
	Total	149.113	224.000				

Take a look at the values of Fstatistic, Sig value (p-value) and F crit presented in the last three columns of above table of ANOVA results. In this experiment, the p-values for sample, columns and interaction are 0.000, 0.949 and 0.035 respectively. Also for sample (Database Systems) and interaction Fstatistics> Fcrit and their corresponding Sig values<0.05. So, I conclude that there is **statistical significant difference in runtimes** w.r.t database systems. I also conclude that the differences between runtimes are likely due to change Database Systems but not due to change in query types.

The plot of means of runtimes for five query statements for three Database Systems (PostgreSQL, SQL and MongoDB) is given in Figure 45 below:

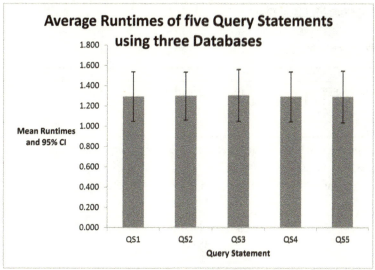

Figure 45: Bar plot of the sample means ±95% CI using all three Databases (Runtimes)

The bar plot of **95% Confidence intervals** of the sample means shown in Figure below:

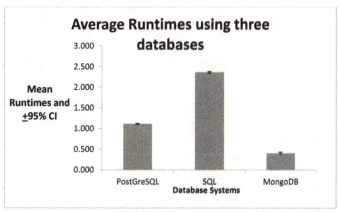

Figure 46: Bar plot of sample means ±95% CI using all three Databases for Runtime

One-way ANOVA

From above evaluation I found significant interaction, that's why I performed one-way ANOVA below to find out the differences between the queries for each DBMS.

For PostgreSQL Database

Anova: Single Factor		POSTGRESQL				
Source of Variation	*SS*	*df*	*MS*	*F*	*P-value*	*F crit*
Between Groups	0.017167288	4	0.004291822	0.83963703	0.504694687	2.502656
Within Groups	0.357806436	70	0.005111521			
Total	0.374973724	74				

Here, p-value>0.05 and also Fstatistic< F crit, so query types do not change using PostgreSQL Database.

The bar plot of five query types using PostgreSQL Database is shown in figure below:

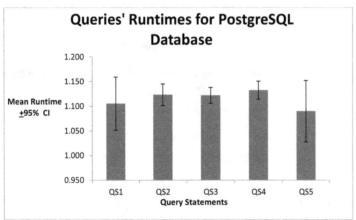

Figure 47: Bar plot sample means ±95% CI using PostgreSQL Database

For SQL Database

Anova: Single Factor		SQL				
Source of Variation	*SS*	*df*	*MS*	*F*	*P-value*	*F crit*
Between Groups	0.083260547	4	0.020815137	2.96208049	0.025470249	2.502656
Within Groups	0.491904108	70	0.007027202			
Total	0.575164655	74				

71

Here, p-value<0.05 and also Fstatistic>F crit, so query types are significant using SQL Database.

The bar plot of five query types using SQL Database is shown in figure below:

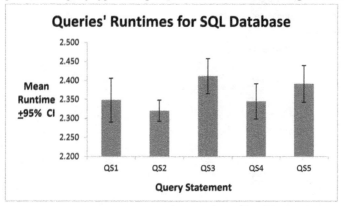

Figure 48: Bar plot of the sample means ±95% CI using SQL Database

For PostgreSQL Database

Anova: Single Factor		MongoDB				
Source of Variation	SS	df	MS	F	P-value	F crit
Between Groups	0.052519666	4	0.013129916	0.95419997	0.438190044	2.502656
Within Groups	0.963209162	70	0.013760131			
Total	1.015728827	74				

Here, p-value>0.05 and also Fstatistic<F crit, so query types do not change using MongoDB Database.

The bar plot of five query types using MongoDB Database is shown in figure below:

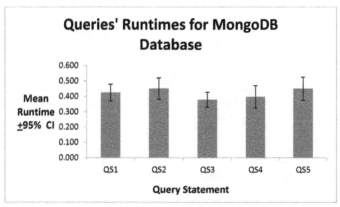

Figure 49: Bar plot of the sample means ±95% CI using MongoDB Database

72

7.2. Analysis of Memory Usage

It can be seen from Table 6 below that there is no or little variance within each group of memory usage. That is the reason I have not applied ANOVA on the datasets to find out the variances for queries' memory usage w.r.t query type complexity and Database System.

MEMORY USAGE

	DataBase Size	1 QS1*	2 QS2*	3 QS3*	4 QS4*	5 QS5*
PostgreSQL	0	25	25	25	25	25
		25	25	25	25	25
		25	25	25	25	25
		25	25	25	25	25
		25	25	25	25	25
	5	26	25	26	25	25
		26	25	26	25	25
		26	25	26	25	25
		26	25	26	25	25
		26	25	26	25	25
	10	27	26	26	25	25
		27	26	26	25	25
		27	26	26	25	25
		27	26	26	25	25
		27	26	26	25	25
SQL	0	0	0	0	0	0
		0	0	0	0	0
		0	0	0	0	0
		0	0	0	0	0
		0	0	0	0	0
	5	2	2	2	2	2
		2	2	2	2	2
		2	2	2	2	2
		2	2	2	2	2
		2	2	2	2	2
	10	3	3	3	3	3
		3	3	3	3	3
		3	3	3	3	3
		3	3	3	3	3
		3	3	3	3	3
MongoDB	0	0	0	0	0	0
		0	0	0	0	0
		0	0	0	0	0
		0	0	0	0	0
		0	0	0	0	0
	5	1.344	0	1.949	2.1	4.172
		1.344	0	1.949	2.1	4.172
		1.344	0	1.949	2.1	4.172
		1.344	0	1.949	2.1	4.172
		1.344	0	1.949	2.1	4.172
	10	2.68	2.04	2.4	2.1	4.172
		2.68	2.04	2.4	2.1	4.172
		2.68	2.04	2.4	2.1	4.172
		2.68	2.04	2.4	2.1	4.172
		2.68	2.04	2.4	2.1	4.172

Table 6: Memory Usage Dataset for all three Databases

Considering the above dataset, I am going to describe memory usage of queries using each database system.

For PostgreSQL Database

Within Data Base Size 0, there is no variance i-e all values are 25.

For larger Data Base Sizes (5 and 10), there is no variance within Queries. Only variance is between the Queries.

In the table below, I have inspected the means for each combination of Query and Data Base Size.

DBSize	QS1*	QS2*	QS3*	QS4*	QS5*	Mean
0	25	25	25	25	25	25
5	26	25	26	25	25	25.4
10	27	26	26	25	25	25.8
Mean	26	25.33333	25.66667	25	25	

Clearly, means are not significant.

For SQL Database

Considering Data for SQL Database, there is no variance within Queries of same Database size.

Also, there is no variance between Queries and only variance is between Database Size. It means larger Database Size consumes more memory.

For MongoDB Database

Within Data Base Size 0, there is no memory usage at all (all values are 0).

For larger Database sizes, there is no variance within Queries. Only variance is between Queries.

I have inspected the means for each combination of Query and Data Base Size below

DBSize	QS1*	QS2*	QS3*	QS4*	QS5*	Mean
0	0	0	0	0	0	0
5	1.34	0	1.95	2.1	4.17	1.912
10	2.68	2.04	2.4	2.1	4.17	2.678
Mean	1.34	0.68	1.45	1.4	2.78	

To sum up all memory usage evaluation considering above analysis, it is obvious that PostgreSQL Database consumes more memory as compared to SQL and MongoDB Databases.

The 3D plot of means of memory usages for five query statements using three Database Systems (PostgreSQL, SQL and MongoDB) is given in Figure 50 below:

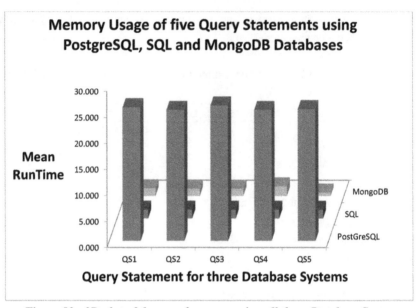

Figure 50: 3D plot of the sample means using all three Database System
(Memory Usage)

8.1. Discussion and Evaluation

In this section, I have agreed and disagreed to various claims regarding RDBMS, ORDBMS and NoSQL Databases Systems.

I agree with (Bloor, 2003) who has claimed that Object Relational DBMSs are faster than RDBMS for transactional purpose. In figure 46 of my report, it is clearly visible that PostgreSQL Database performs much faster than SQL Database in terms of speed (runtime).

(Hadjigeorgiou, 2013) performed certain tests for simple query with different database sizes up to 10000 using MySQL and MongoDB Databases. He has claimed that with increase in database size, MongoDB shows no significant variance whereas MySQL shows little variations with increase in time when DB Size increases. I completely agree because in my project, it is clear and obvious that Database size doesn't affect the performance using three DBMSs (section 7.1.1)

I was thinking to design, model and implement NOSQL system keeping ERD in my mind that is a relational schema, this was the major issue I faced while moving from RDBMS to NoSQL Solution. I agree with (Stanier, 2012) who has claimed that it is a chaotic situation and major fault to keep ERD in mind while designing and modelling NoSQL solutions.

According to (Hadjigeorgiou, 2013), in case the complex query that contains two JOINS MongoDB Database has advantage over MySQL Database due to its use of embedded (nested) JSON documents. I agree because in my project query 4 has joins and in MongoDB I implemented this query using embedding approach. From statistical results it is clear that MongoDB Database shows much faster performance than SQL Database for query 4.

I disagree with (Chorzow, 2010) who has claimed that MongoDB is schema-less. Somehow, it is true that there is no proper schema for MongoDB because the database can vary with change in time and requirements. That's why NoSQL solutions are flexible. But, user can design schemas according to the needs like I did. In my report, I presented self-designed schema for MongoDB database. I have designed the schema using both referencing and embedding of data.

I agree with (Han et al., 2011) who has claimed that NoSQL Databases are open source and therefore there are no costs of hardware and/or licenses like a few relational databases. In my project, at first I implemented Airline Information System using Oracle 11g that is licenced because I have been given with credentials from university but I don't have proper privileges, due to this issue I had to implement my case study again in SQL Server because I had to record queries' memory usage and in Oracle 11g I couldn't do so without license.

According to (Technirvanaa.wordpress.com, 2011), most designers and developers are at ease with RDBMS concepts and techniques. I agree because as I have already mentioned above that I was designing NoSQL solution keeping relational schema in my mind.

(MongoDB vs. SQL Server 2008 Performance Showdown, 2010) has claimed that MongoDB performs 100 times better than SQL Server. I agree because it is clearly shown in figure 46 that MongoDB is much faster than SQL Server.

(Nichols, 2007) has claimed that relational joins take much more time to query data as compared to object references. I agree and it is clearly visible in figure 46 that PostgreSQL database performs faster that SQL Server.

8.2. Conclusion

From section 7.1.1, no statistical differences have been found in performance w.r.t DB size using each of the three database systems. Hence, I conclude that there is no statistical **significant difference in performance (in terms of runtime and memory usage)** w.r.t DB Size using each of the three database systems. Therefore, I accept first Null Hypothesis (H_0) i-e

H_0: There is NO (significant) difference in performance (in terms of speed (runtime) and memory usage) w.r.t Database Size using each of the three database systems i-e Object-Relational (PostgreSQL) DBMS, Relational (SQL) DBMS and Document-Oriented NoSQL (Mongo dB) DBMS.**OR** There is NO (significant) difference in the means of the runtime and memory usage w.r.t Database Size i-e $\mu 1= \mu 2= \mu 3.$

However, 7.1.2 presents all Fstatistics>Fcrit and also p-values<0.05. Therefore, I conclude that there are statistical **significant differences in performance (in terms of runtime and memory usage)** w.r.t query type complexity and Database Systems. Hence, I accept second Alternative Hypothesis (H_A) i-e

H_A: There is a (significant) difference in performance (in terms of speed (runtime) and memory usage) w.r.t query type complexity between three database systems

Object-Relational (PostgreSQL) DBMS, Relational (SQL) DBMS and Document-Oriented NoSQL (MongoDB) DBMS.

OR There is a (significant) difference in the means of runtime and memory usage i-e $\mu1 \neq \mu2 \neq \mu3$.

On the other hand, after finding significant differences I performed One-Way ANOVA w.r.t query type complexity for each of the three database systems separately. Sections 7.1.2 presents Fstatistics>Fcrit and also p-values<0.05 for SQL Database. Hence, I conclude that there are statistical **significant differences in performance (in terms of runtime and memory usage)** w.r.t query type complexity and accept third Alternative Hypothesis $(\mathbf{H_A})$ i-e

$\mathbf{H_A}$: There is a (significant) difference in performance (in terms of speed (runtime) and memory usage) w.r.t query type complexity using each of the three database systems Object-Relational (PostgreSQL) DBMS, Relational (SQL) DBMS and Document-Oriented NoSQL (MongoDB) DBMS.

OR There is (significant) difference in the means of runtime and memory usage w.r.t query type complexity i-e $\mu1 \neq \mu2 \neq \mu3 \neq \mu4 \neq \mu5$.

Clearly from figure 45, figure 46 and figure 50, it can be seen that MongoDB is fastest Database in performance (in terms of speed (runtime) and memory usage). On the other hand, SQL Database is slowest in terms of speed and PostgreSQL Database is worst in memory consumption.

So, in order to address the research question of this report, I will conclude my report with the following statement:

Yes, there are significant differences in performance (in terms of speed (runtime) and memory usage) w.r.t query type complexity irrespective of DB Size between Object-Relational DBMS (PostgreSql), Relational DBMS (SQL) and Document-Oriented NoSQL (Mongo dB) DBMS.

8.3 Future Research

I tested performance of databases for 10 numbers of records, from a few aspects using three databases. There are lots and lots of additional research that can be done. For future research, I suggest following tasks:

- Additional data (Big Data).

- Use some other database systems like CouchDB, key-value stores or other NoSQL databases etc.
- More functions of the databases, such as sharding and replication in MongoDB.
- Other features of the performance, such as consistency and availability.
- Other types of queries and data models.
- Insertion of data using programing languages in MongoDB like Java, C++ etc.

Bibliography:

Elmasri, R. (2011). Fundamentals of database systems. 6th ed. [eBook] Available at:
http://www.cvauni.edu.vn/imgupload_dinhkem/file/CSDL/Fundamentals_of_Database_Systems,_6th_Edition.pdf [Accessed 2 Jun. 2014].

w3resource, (2014). NoSQL introduction - w3resource. [Online] Available at:
http://www.w3resource.com/mongodb/nosql.php [Accessed 3 Jun. 2014].

Convertdb.com, (2014). MS SQL to PostgreSQL Migration and Sync.
[Online] Available at: http://convertdb.com/mssql/postgresql [Accessed 3 Jun. 2014].

Postgresqltutorial.com, (2014). What is PostgreSQL [online] Available at:
http://www.postgresqltutorial.com/what-is-postgresql/ [Accessed 3 Jun. 2014].

Webopedia.com, (2014). What is Database (DB)? Webopedia [online] Available at:
http://www.webopedia.com/TERM/D/database.html [Accessed 3 Jun. 2014].

Databasedir.com, (2014). What is RDBMS? - Database Directory. [Online]
Available at: http://www.databasedir.com/what-is-rdbms/ [Accessed 3 Jun. 2014].

Pgadmin.org, (2014). PgAdmin: PostgreSQL administration and management
tools. [Online] Available at: http://www.pgadmin.org/ [Accessed 30 Jun. 2014].

Aircraft-registration-country-codes.blogspot.co.uk, (2014). Aircraft Registration
Country Codes / Prefixes. [Online] Available at: http://aircraft-registration-country-codes.blogspot.co.uk/ [Accessed 30 Jun. 2014].

Airlinecodes.co.uk, (2014). The Airline Codes Website. [Online] Available at:
http://www.airlinecodes.co.uk/arctypes.asp#L [Accessed 30 Jun. 2014].

Flightradar24.com, (2014). Flights database - Flightradar24. [Online] Available at:
http://www.flightradar24.com/data/flights/ [Accessed 30 Jun. 2014].

Postgresql.org, (2014). PostgreSQL: Documentation: 8.3: Resource Consumption.
[Online] Available at: http://www.postgresql.org/docs/8.3/static/runtime-config-resource.html [Accessed 30 Jun. 2014].

Mongodb.com, (2014). The database market is in play | MongoDB. [Online]
Available at: http://www.mongodb.com/post/35653616737/the-database-market-is-in-play [Accessed 1 Jul. 2014]

Contributor, G. (2012). Migrating from a relational to a NoSQL cloud database.
[Online] TechRepublic. Available at: http://www.techrepublic.com/blog/the-enterprise-cloud/migrating-from-a-relational-to-a-nosql-cloud-database/ [Accessed 1 Jul. 2014].

Li, Y. and Manoharan, S. (2013). A performance comparison of SQL and NoSQL databases. Communications, Computers and Signal Processing (PACRIM), 2013 IEEE Pacific Rim Conference on, [online] pp.15-19. Available at: http://ieeexplore.ieee.org/xpls/icp.jsp?arnumber=6625441 [Accessed 1 Jul. 2014].

Warden, P. (2011). Big data glossary. 1st ed. Sebastopol, CA: O'Reilly.

Han, J., Haihong, E., Le, G. and Du, J. (2011). Survey on NoSQL database. Pervasive Computing and Applications (ICPCA), 2011 6th International Conference on, [online] pp.363-366. Available at: http://ieeexplore.ieee.org/stamp/stamp.jsp?tp=&arnumber=6106531 [Accessed 2 Jul. 2014].

Syoncloud.com, (2014). Overview of Big Data and NoSQL Technologies as of January 2013 | Syoncloud. [Online] Available at: http://www.syoncloud.com/big_data_technology_overview [Accessed 2 Jul. 2014].

Mongodb.com, (2014). NoSQL Databases Explained | MongoDB. [Online] Available at: http://www.mongodb.com/nosql-explained [Accessed 2 Jul. 2014].

Greene, N. (2014). [Blog] Available at: http://greendatacenterconference.com/blog/the-five-key-advantages-and-disadvantages-of-nosql/ [Accessed 2 Jul. 2014].

Technirvanaa.wordpress.com, (2011). NoSql disadvantages | Tech Nirvana. [Online] Available at: https://technirvanaa.wordpress.com/tag/nosql-disadvantages/ [Accessed 2 Jul. 2014].

Nayak, A., Poriya, A. and Poojary, D. (2013). Type of NOSQL Databases and its Comparison with Relational Databases. International Journal of Applied Information Systems (IJAIS), [online] 5(4), p.4. Available at: http://research.ijais.org/volume5/number4/ijais12-450888.pdf [Accessed 2 Jul. 2014].

Roijackers, J. (2014). Bridging SQL and NoSQL. Masters. Eindhoven University of Technology.

Meijer, E. and Bierman, G. (n.d). "A co-relational model of data for large shared data banks," Queue, vol. 9, no. 3, pp. 30:30–30:48, Mar. 2011. [Online] Available at: http://delivery.acm.org/10.1145/1970000/1961297/p30-meijer.pdf?ip=147.197.251.157&id=1961297&acc=OPEN&key=BF07A2EE685417C5%2E3BD3653AA34A5633%2E4D4702B0C3E38B35%2E6D218144511F3437&CFID=497775177&CFTOKEN=79555651&__acm__=1404299623_838e2e7259a16309f508db086dfdad92 [Accessed 2 Jul. 2014].

Bartholomew, D. (2010). SQL vs. NoSQL. Linux Journal, [online] 2010(195), p.4. Available at: http://www.linuxjournal.com/article/10770. [Accessed 2 Jul. 2014].

Sakr, S., Liu, A., Batista, D. and Alomari, M. (2011). A survey of large scale data management approaches in cloud environments. Communications Surveys \& Tutorials, IEEE, 13(3), pp.311--336. [Online] Available at: http://www.nicta.com.au/pub?doc=4784 [Accessed 2 Jul. 2014].

Varley, I. (2009). No Relation: The Mixed Blessings of Non-Relational Databases. Masters. The University of Texas at Austin. [online] Available at: http://ianvarley.com/UT/MR/Varley_MastersReport_Full_2009-08-07.pdf[Accessed 2 Jul. 2014].

Stonebraker, m. (2010). SQL Databases v. noSQL Databases. [Blog] CommuniCAtionS of thE ACm. Available at: http://delivery.acm.org/10.1145/1730000/1721659/p10-stonebraker.pdf?ip=147.197.251.157&id=1721659&acc=ACTIVE%20SERVICE&key=BF07A2EE685417C5%2E3BD3653AA34A5633%2E4D4702B0C3E38B35%2E4D4702B0C3E38B35&CFID=497775177&CFTOKEN=79555651&__acm__=1404301915_d1b091f0e268692ca7ac403d19dad46b [Accessed 2 Jul. 2014].

Cattell, R. (2011). Scalable SQL and NoSQL data stores. ACM SIGMOD Record, [online] 39(4), pp.12--27. Available at: http://www.sigmod.org/publications/sigmod-record/1012/pdfs/04.surveys.cattell.pdf [Accessed 2 Jul. 2014].

MongoDB vs. SQL Server 2008 Performance Showdown. (2010). [Blog] Michael Kennedy on Technology. Available at: http://blog.michaelckennedy.net/2010/04/29/mongodb-vs-sql-server-2008-performance-showdown/ [Accessed 18 Aug. 2014].

Cooper, B., Silberstein, A., Tam, E., Ramakrishnan, R. and Sears, R. (2010). Benchmarking cloud serving systems with YCSB. [online] pp.143--154. Available at: http://delivery.acm.org/10.1145/1810000/1807152/p143-cooper.pdf?ip=147.197.251.157&id=1807152&acc=ACTIVE%20SERVICE&key=BF07A2EE685417C5%2E3BD3653AA34A5633%2E4D4702B0C3E38B35%2E4D4702B0C3E38B35&CFID=497775177&CFTOKEN=79555651&__acm__=1404302937_3dc28858407b035d5257722473e8fa9e [Accessed 2 Jul. 2014].

Nichols, L. (2007). A COMPARISON OF OBJECT-RELATIONAL AND RELATIONAL DATABASES. Masters. California Polytechnic State University [Online] Available at: http://users.csc.calpoly.edu/~gfisher/classes/590/reference/theses/nichols.pdf [Accessed 5 Sep. 2014].

Codd, E. (1970). A Relational Model of Data for Large Shared Data Banks. [Online] Available at: http://www.seas.upenn.edu/~zives/03f/cis550/codd.pdf [Accessed 5 Sep. 2014].

Silberschatz, A., F. Korth, H. and Sudarshan, S. (2011). Database System Concepts. 6th ed. [ebook] New York. [Online] Available at: http://fit.hcmute.edu.vn/web/phuongn/3;jsessionid=17C07A6206394D05BF87677C33 A437F6?p_p_id=19&p_p_lifecycle=1&p_p_state=exclusive&p_p_mode=view&_19_ struts_action=%2Fmessage_boards%2Fget_message_attachment&_19_messageId=18 0957&_19_attachment=Database+System+Concepts.pdf [Accessed 2 Sep. 2014]. (Sqlcourse.com, 2014)

Sqlcourse.com, (2014). SQLCourse - Lesson 1: What is SQL?. [online] Available at: http://www.sqlcourse.com/intro.html [Accessed 5 Sep. 2014].

Techopedia.com, (2014). What is Structured Query Language (SQL)? - Definition from Techopedia. [online] Available at: http://www.techopedia.com/definition/1245/structured-query-language-sql [Accessed 5 Sep. 2014].

Docs.oracle.com, (2014). History of SQL. [Online] Available at: http://docs.oracle.com/cd/B12037_01/server.101/b10759/intro001.htm [Accessed 5 Sep. 2014].

Wang, M. (2010). USING OBJECT-RELATIONAL DATABASE TECHNOLOGY TO SOLVE PROBLEMS IN DATABASE DEVELOPMENT. [online] 11(1). Available at: http://iacis.org/iis/2010/90-99_LV2010_1543.pdf [Accessed 5 Sep. 2014].

Vasiliev, A. (2013). World of the NoSQL databases. [Blog] Leopard Blog. Available at: http://leopard.in.ua/2013/11/08/nosql-world/ [Accessed 5 Sep. 2014].

Alex, Sydney, and Shubha, (n.d.). [Online] Available at: http://www.cs.sjsu.edu/faculty/kim/cs157b/contents/presentations/slides/Comparison_ of_NOSQL_Solutions.pdf [Accessed 5 Sep. 2014].

Burd, G. (2011). NoSQL. [online] 36(5). Available at: https://www.usenix.org/legacy/publications/login/2011-10/openpdfs/Burd.pdf [Accessed 18 Aug. 2014]

Edlich, P. (2014). NOSQL Databases. [online] Nosql-database.org. Available at: http://nosql-database.org/ [Accessed 16 Aug. 2014].

Education Portal, (2014). What is a Database Management System? - Purpose and Function Video - Lesson and Example | Education Portal. [online] Available at:

http://education-portal.com/academy/lesson/what-is-a-database-management-system-purpose-and-function.html#lesson [Accessed 6 Sep. 2014].

Sadalage, P. and Fowler, M. (2013). NoSQL Distilled. 1st ed. [eBook] Available at:
http://ptgmedia.pearsoncmg.com/images/9780321826626/samplepages/0321826620.pdf [Accessed 17 Aug. 2014].

Bloor, R. (2003). The Failure of Relational Database, The Rise of Object Technology and the Need for the Hybrid Database. [online] Available at:
http://www.intersystems.com/assets/baroudi_bloor.pdf [Accessed 6 Sep. 2014].

Connolly, T. and Begg, C. (2002). Database systems. 1st ed. Harlow, England: Addison-Wesley.

McNulty, E. (2014). SQL vs. NoSQL- What You Need to Know - Dataconomy. [online] Dataconomy.com. Available at: http://dataconomy.com/sql-vs-nosql-need-know/ [Accessed 6 Sep. 2014].

Stajano, F. (1998). A Gentle Introduction to Relational and Object Oriented Databases. [online] ORL. Available at: https://www.cl.cam.ac.uk/~fms27/db/tr-98-2.pdf [Accessed 7 Sep. 2014].

Ji-feng, Z. and Zhi-yong, P. (2004). SQL3 object model and its extension. Wuhan University Journal of Natural Sciences, 9(5), pp.681--686.

SAB\uAU, G. (2007). Comparison of RDBMS, OODBMS and ORDBMS. Revista InformaticaEconomic\ua,(44).

Leavitt, N. (2000). Whatever happened to object-oriented databases?. Computer, 33(8), pp.16--19.

Egenhofer, M. and U. Frank, A. (1992). Object-Oriented Modelling for GIS. URISA, [online] 4(2). Available at:
http://www.spatial.maine.edu/~max/oomodeling.pdf [Accessed 6 Sep. 2014].

LBS kuttipedia, (2013). SIMPLE ER DIAGRAM ON AIRLINE DATABASE(S5 CS2 ROLL NO 16). [online] Available at:
http://lbsitbytes2010.wordpress.com/2013/09/25/simple-er-diagram-on-airline-databases5-cs2-roll-no-16/ [Accessed 9 Sep. 2014].

Academic2.strose.edu, (2014). CHAPTER 3: DATA MODELING USING THE ENTITY-RELATIONSHIP MODEL. [online] Available at:
http://academic2.strose.edu/Math_And_Science/avitabij/cis503fall06/answers3.htm [Accessed 9 Sep. 2014].

SÖDERGREN, P. and Englund, B. (2011). Investigating NoSQL from a SQL Perspective.

Chapple, M. (2014). Everything You Need to Know about the ACID Model: Database Theory. [online] About. Available at: http://databases.about.com/od/specificproducts/a/acid.htm [Accessed 9 Sep. 2014].

Pritchett, D. (2008). Base: An acid alternative. Queue, 6(3), pp.48--55.

Gilbert, S. and Lynch, N. (2012). Perspectives on the CAP Theorem.

Hurst, N. (2014). Visual Guide to NoSQL Systems. [Blog] Nathan Hurst's Blog. Available at: http://blog.nahurst.com/visual-guide-to-nosql-systems [Accessed 10 Sep. 2014].

Hadjigeorgiou, C. (2013). RDBMS vs NoSQL: Performance and Scaling Comparison.

Mongodb.org, (2014). MongoDB. [online] Available at: http://www.mongodb.org/ [Accessed 10 Sep. 2014].

Mongodb.com, (2014). MongoDB Overview. [online] Available at: http://www.mongodb.com/mongodb-overview [Accessed 11 Sep. 2014].

Aruizca.com, (2014). [online] Available at: http://aruizca.com/content/images/MongoDB-talk/MongoDB_files/t5VI8Mo.png [Accessed 11 Sep. 2014].

Chodorow, K. & Dirolf, M. (2010). MongoDB: The Definitive Guide. 1st ed. Sebastopol, CA: O'Reilly Media.

Controls.engin.umich.edu, (2014). Factor analysis and ANOVA - ControlsWiki. [online] Available at: https://controls.engin.umich.edu/wiki/index.php/Factor_analysis_and_ANOVA [Accessed 12 Sep. 2014].

Aquafold.com, (2014). Aqua Data Studio : Tool to develop, access, manage and visually analyze data. [online] Available at: http://www.aquafold.com/aquadatastudio.html [Accessed 13 Sep. 2014].

Whatis.techtarget.com, (2014). What is 3Vs (volume, variety and velocity) ? - Definition from WhatIs.com. [online] Available at: http://whatis.techtarget.com/definition/3Vs [Accessed 14 Sep. 2014].

Stanier, C. (2012). Introducing NoSQL into the Database Curriculum. p.61.

Appendices:

Appendix 1: Measurement of Queries' Runtime and Memory Usage for PostgreSQL (Dataset)

Query #	Number of Records	Run #	Time (ms)	Memory (kb)
1	0	1	14	25
1	0	2	12	25
1	0	3	13	25
1	0	4	12	25
1	0	5	11	25
1	5	1	11	26
1	5	2	13	26
1	5	3	11	26
1	5	4	12	26
1	5	5	13	26
1	10	1	13	26
1	10	2	12	26
1	10	3	13	26
1	10	4	12	26
1	10	5	12	26
2	0	1	13	25
2	0	2	12	25
2	0	3	13	25
2	0	4	12	25
2	0	5	11	25
2	5	1	12	25
2	5	2	12	25
2	5	3	12	25
2	5	4	14	25
2	5	5	12	25
2	10	1	12	25
2	10	2	14	25
2	10	3	13	25
2	10	4	15	25
2	10	5	12	25
3	0	1	11	25
3	0	2	12	25
3	0	3	12	25

3	0	4	11	25
3	0	5	14	25
3	5	1	14	26
3	5	2	13	26
3	5	3	12	26
3	5	4	14	26
3	5	5	11	26
3	10	1	12	27
3	10	2	14	27
3	10	3	12	27
3	10	4	13	27
3	10	5	5	27
4	0	1	12	25
4	0	2	11	25
4	0	3	14	25
4	0	4	12	25
4	0	5	12	25
4	5	1	13	25
4	5	2	13	25
4	5	3	12	25
4	5	4	4	25
4	5	5	12	25
4	10	1	13	25
4	10	2	11	25
4	10	3	11	25
4	10	4	11	25
4	10	5	13	25
5	0	1	12	25
5	0	2	13	25
5	0	3	13	25
5	0	4	14	25
5	0	5	12	25
5	5	1	12	25
5	5	2	13	25
5	5	3	15	25
5	5	4	11	25
5	5	5	11	25
5	10	1	11	26
5	10	2	13	26
5	10	3	13	26
5	10	4	11	26

| 5 | 10 | 5 | 11 | 26 |

Appendix 2: Measurement of Queries' Runtime and Memory Usage for SQL (Dataset)

Query #	Number of Records	Run #	Time (ms)	Memory (kb)
1	0	1	263	0
1	0	2	248	0
1	0	3	191	0
1	0	4	205	0
1	0	5	217	0
1	5	1	386	2
1	5	2	300	2
1	5	3	251	2
1	5	4	230	2
1	5	5	218	2
1	10	1	314	3
1	10	2	280	3
1	10	3	331	3
1	10	4	254	3
1	10	5	236	3
2	0	1	310	0
2	0	2	208	0
2	0	3	195	0
2	0	4	185	0
2	0	5	197	0
2	5	1	304	2
2	5	2	232	2
2	5	3	185	2
2	5	4	193	2
2	5	5	305	2
2	10	1	204	3
2	10	2	259	3
2	10	3	190	3
2	10	4	184	3
2	10	5	215	3
3	0	1	291	0
3	0	2	174	0
3	0	3	184	0
3	0	4	196	0

3	0	5	192	0
3	5	1	267	2
3	5	2	217	2
3	5	3	190	2
3	5	4	200	2
3	5	5	193	2
3	10	1	265	3
3	10	2	209	3
3	10	3	208	3
3	10	4	193	3
3	10	5	289	3
4	0	1	365	0
4	0	2	205	0
4	0	3	196	0
4	0	4	215	0
4	0	5	298	0
4	5	1	343	2
4	5	2	214	2
4	5	3	241	2
4	5	4	214	2
4	5	5	261	2
4	10	1	289	3
4	10	2	282	3
4	10	3	199	3
4	10	4	210	3
4	10	5	219	3
5	0	1	221	0
5	0	2	177	0
5	0	3	197	0
5	0	4	190	0
5	0	5	198	0
5	5	1	198	2
5	5	2	204	2
5	5	3	196	2
5	5	4	203	2
5	5	5	282	2
5	10	1	251	3
5	10	2	192	3
5	10	3	213	3
5	10	4	216	3
5	10	5	202	3

Appendix 3: Measurement of Queries' Runtime and Memory Usage for MongoDB (Dataset)

Query #	Number of Records	Run #	Time (ms)	Memory (kb)
1	0	1	2	0
1	0	2	1	0
1	0	3	2	0
1	0	4	1	0
1	0	5	1	0
1	5	1	68	1.949
1	5	2	2	1.949
1	5	3	1	1.949
1	5	4	1	1.949
1	5	5	2	1.949
1	10	1	1	2.4
1	10	2	1	2.4
1	10	3	2	2.4
1	10	4	1	2.4
1	10	5	2	2.4
2	0	1	2	0
2	0	2	1	0
2	0	3	12	0
2	0	4	2	0
2	0	5	2	0
2	5	1	164	2.1
2	5	2	2	2.1
2	5	3	2	2.1
2	5	4	1	2.1
2	5	5	2	2.1
2	10	1	48	2.1
2	10	2	2	2.1
2	10	3	1	2.1
2	10	4	2	2.1
2	10	5	0	2.1
3	0	1	1	0
3	0	2	2	0
3	0	3	2	0
3	0	4	2	0
3	0	5	1	0
3	5	1	1	1.344

3	5	2	3	1.344
3	5	3	2	1.344
3	5	4	13	1.344
3	5	5	1	1.344
3	10	1	2	2.68
3	10	2	2	2.68
3	10	3	2	2.68
3	10	4	2	2.68
3	10	5	1	2.68
4	0	1	0	0
4	0	2	2	0
4	0	3	2	0
4	0	4	1	0
4	0	5	2	0
4	5	1	2	2.78
4	5	2	2	2.78
4	5	3	2	2.78
4	5	4	2	2.78
4	5	5	1	2.78
4	10	1	2	2.78
4	10	2	1	2.78
4	10	3	2	2.78
4	10	4	1	2.78
4	10	5	1	2.78
5	0	1	2	0
5	0	2	3	0
5	0	3	1	0
5	0	4	4	0
5	0	5	2	0
5	5	1	2	0
5	5	2	1	0
5	5	3	1	0
5	5	4	2	0
5	5	5	2	0
5	10	1	1	2.04
5	10	2	2	2.04
5	10	3	3	2.04
5	10	4	2	2.04
5	10	5	1	2.04